What Happens When We Pray & Believe GOD

Leonard MP Kayiwa

Unless otherwise indicated, all Scripture quotations are taken from the
New King James version of the Bible,
and the old King James version

Formatted and typed by:
Pastor Gail B. Kayiwa, D.D.

Cover Design and Illustrations by:
Dr. Leonard Kayiwa
kayiwaministries@yahoo.com

What Happens When We Pray and Believe God
ISBN 978-0-9717609-1-2
Copyright ©2016 by Leonard MP Kayiwa

All rights reserved. Written permission must
Be secured from the publisher to use or
Reproduce any part of this book, except for
Brief quotations in critical reviews or
Articles.

Printed in the United States of America

Leonard Kayiwa Ministries
P.O. Box 1898
Bolingbrook, Illinois 60440

Dedication

THIS BOOK IS DEDICATED
TO THE PEOPLE
IN
AFRICA, AMERICA
EUROPE, CHINA,
AUSTRALIA,
MIDDLE EAST, ETC.,
AND
TO ALL CHURCHES
AROUND THE WORLD
PLUS,
THOSE WHO HAVE WORKED
WITH ME
TO MAKE THE BOOK AVAILABLE
TO THE
NATIONS:
MY WIFE, DR. GAIL B. KAYIWA
AND MY CHILDREN
MOSES EMMANUEL KAYIWA
JOSHUA ISRAEL KAYIWA
ENOCH DEOGRACIOUS KAYIWA,
AND
MARY DEBORAH NAKAYIWA

ENDORSEMENTS

Prayer is a very vital part in the life of a believer for it is God Himself who invites us to fellowship with Him through act of prayer. This book addresses the very core of what happens when a human being reaches out to God, believing that God hears. The testimonies and Bible scriptures that the author has quoted in the various chapters in this book helps the believer to desire to pray more, knowing that great things happen when we pray and believe God. Thank God for Apostle/Pastor Leonard Kayiwa having obeyed the Lord God Almighty to share such wonderful revelation with the Body of Christ and individuals worldwide.

Pastor Davis

This is a delightful and refreshing book that I highly recommend to the Body of Christ. It is a must read!!! This book is a game changer.

Evangelist Grace

We thank God almighty for enabling our brother in Christ Leonard Kayiwa to write such an inspiring book. A book that literally revitalizes one's faith and causes someone to see possibilities in God. This man of God, born in Uganda, Africa, now a citizen of the United States of America, has shared with us amazing testimonies of God's supernatural acts, In the Bible, and in the church today through the pages of this power packed, anointed book, "What happens when we pray and believe God." This is a must read. Get the book and recommend it to all of your friends.

BISHOP TODD

This book is a must read! You won't be able to put it down, once you start reading it. Thank God for this book.

BROTHER SAM HONNOLD

This book is a faith booster, out of it radiates revelation knowledge on every page. As the author graciously under the anointing enables you to see beyond the veil and get a glimpse of what happens when we pray and believe God. Thank God for Bishop Leonard Kayiwa's obedience to put together this book that will bless churches and lives for years to come. Personally, I have been greatly blessed by reading this book.

DR. GAIL B. KAYIWA, B.A., M.A., PROFESSIONAL GRANT WRITER

mrsrev3@gmail.com

FORWARD

IT IS TIME TO MIX THE WORD OF GOD YOU HEAR WITH FAITH

Faith is a very important ingredient in a Believer/Church life. With faith, we please God and also receive a good report.

A Believer/church that acknowledges that God is; and Him and His word are one; as well as take time to hear, and confess the Word of God, ends up established on a solid rock—Jesus Christ.

That believer/church can't lack good works, and with faith so much is accomplished, along with receiving the promises of God in His word.

"For indeed the gospel was preached to us as well as to them; but the word which they heard did not profit them, not being mixed with faith in those who heard it. For we who have believed do enter that rest………"Hebrews 4:2-3

This book enables you to see beyond the natural veil and walks you through the behind the scene workings of God in numerous examples in the Bible, as well as testimonies of God's working to cause prayer to be answered.

As you read through these pages, radiant with revelation knowledge, by the Holy Spirit, your faith will increase more and more, as well as the church to which you attend or minister, and great exploits will be wrought for God through your life/church.

"Thus says the Lord, your Redeemer, The Holy One of Israel: I am the Lord your God, Who teaches you to profit, Who leads you by the way you should go." Isaiah 48:17 This book is a gem, a treasure, a pearl of great price in your hands. Read every page prayerfully.

Your Brother in Christ;

Bishop Leonard Kayiwa

DR. BISHOP LEONARD MP KAYIWA

ABOUT THE AUTHOR

Dr. Leonard Kayiwa is a highly anointed servant of God, he started ministering before the Lord, early in life. An altar boy at nine years old, he served at St. Peter's Cathedral at Sambya, Kampala, Uganda, Africa. He would serve in every mass, almost every day.

His love for God began early. After finishing primary school at St. Peter's Primary, he joined St. Henry's College Kitovu, Masaka, Uganda, where God blessed him with very high marks in school, whereby he could devote a lot of his time helping his fellow students in whatever subject needed help in. God gifted him, especially in mathematics, physics, chemistry, history, technical drawing and Biblical studies.

He joined Makerere University in Kampala, Uganda where "he got born again", which resulted in a drastic change in his life. He did Irrigation and Water Conservation Engineering at Hahai University in Nanjing, China and received the Baptism of the Holy Spirit with evidence of speaking in tongues in Hong Kong, at the new Covenant Church. God does unusual miracles through his life and many have become "born again" through his ministry.

TABLE OF CONTENTS

(1) Foundational Truth I   17
    Know You can Ask What You Will

(2) Foundational Truth II   31
    Have Faith in God

(3) Foundational Truth III   59
    God Wants to Show Himself Great on Your Behalf

(4) Foundational Truth IV   87
    As This Happens when we Pray and Believe God

(5) Foundational Truth V   109
    Is the Same Yesterday, Today and Forever

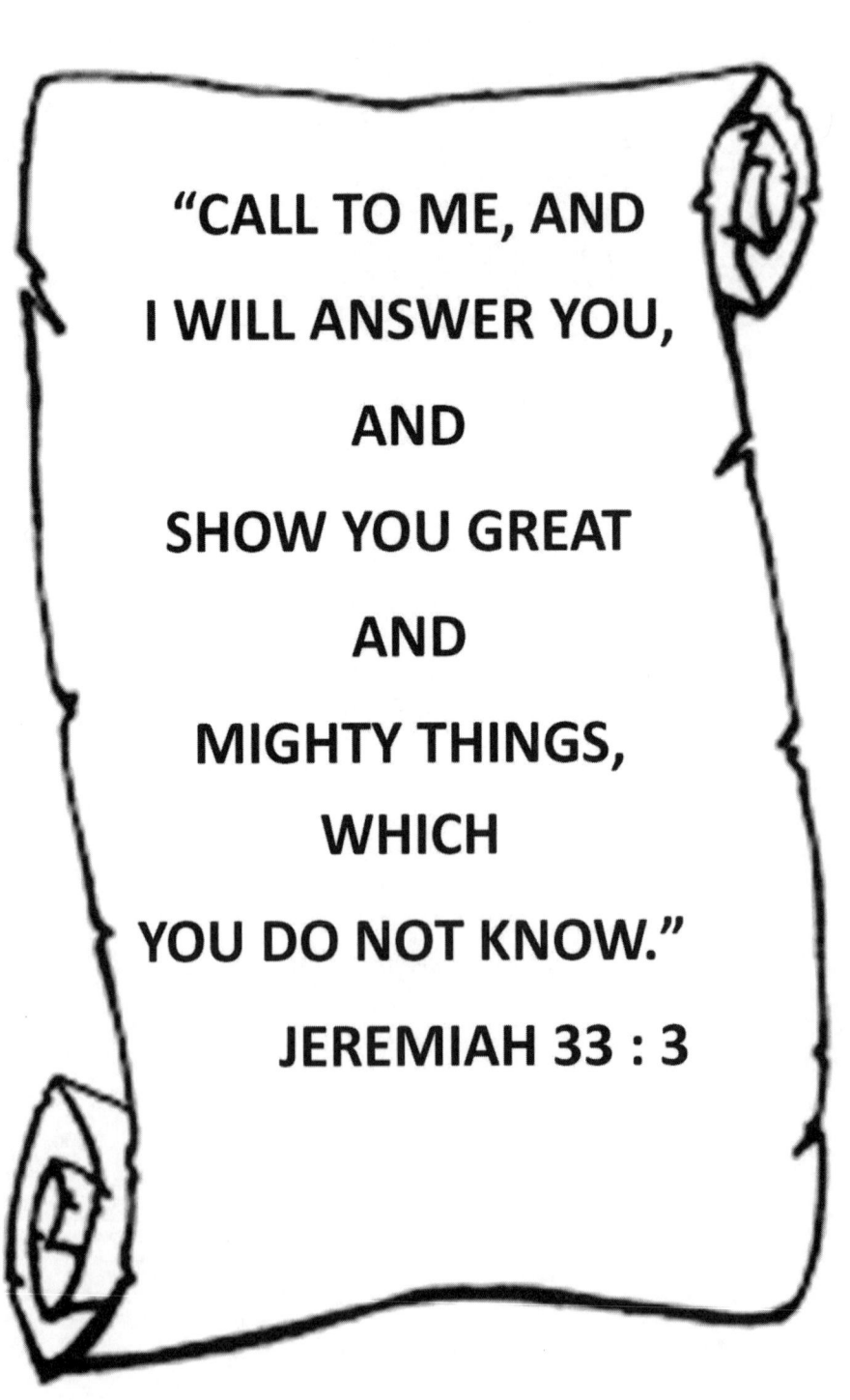

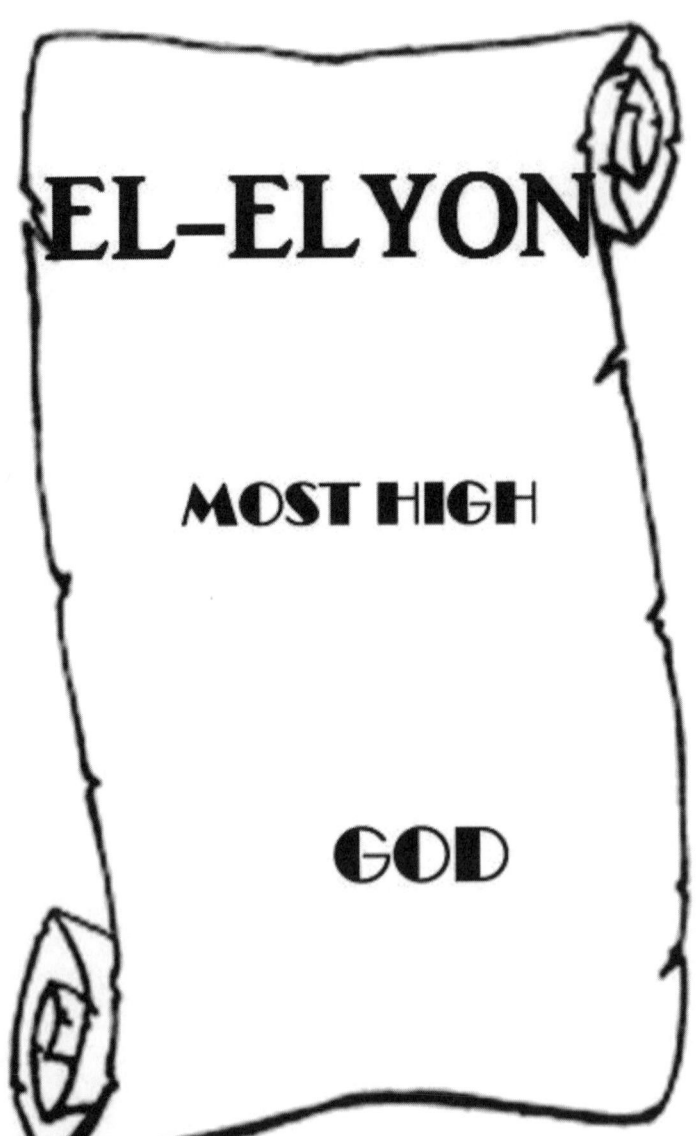

1

FOUNDATIONAL TRUTH 1

KNOW YOU CAN ASK WHAT YOU WILL

"If ye abide in Me, and My words abide in you, you will ask what you desire, and it shall be done for you." (John 15:7)

Abiding in God

Preaching and teaching of the Word by the grace of God as I pastored in the various churches, God enabled me to minister in, I have run into some of the challenges which God's people encounter in their journey with the Lord.

Some even wonder if one can ask what they will from God and God grants it.

It is very important to have knowledge in regard to this aspect of faith, for it's foundational in what you are about to experience in this book, concerning what

What Happens When We Pray And Believe God

happens when we pray and believe God. Even as I am bringing this revelation, right now your faith is being boosted, for the entrance of His words gives light, *"The entrance of Your words gives light."* Psalm 119:130.

It is God's will for us believers to abide in Him by living the new life we received when we got born again, a life of communing with God.

We need to realize that God in the person of the Holy Spirit is in us, then we should flow along with Him as He leads us: "For as many as are led by the Spirit of God, these are the sons of God," Romans 8:14.

The Spirit of God bears witness with our spirit that we are sons of God. When we live as the Spirit tells us and having our minds filled by what the Spirit wants us to have, we abide in God.

Word Abiding In You

God wills his word to abide in us because it is life to those who find it. We need to give God's word a first place in our lives for through it we get to know his

Know You Can Ask What You Will

will.

I have come across a number of folks bothered with (1 John 5:14-15), "Now this is the confidence that we have in Him, that if we ask anything according to His will, He hears us. And if we know that He hears us, whatever we ask, we know that we have the petitions that we have asked of Him."

God's will is found in his word. We need to read/listen/attend to his word which is life to those who receive it. So by getting his word in us, we get to know his will. Therefore, to pray according to the will of God as well as living as he wills, his word must abide in us.

You Shall Ask Whatever You Will

You shall, follows the observance of the first two conditions. It is a sure move, it is an authorizing kind of saying, that now it is all right, in order to ….

When we abide in God and His word abides in us "You Shall" just follows automatically, that's action.

As we live according to the first two standards, we get

What Happens When We Pray And Believe God

to clearly see the immeasurable blessings we have in God through Christ and start acting.

When we abide in God and his word abides in us, God's will becomes our will, so that what you will actually is what God wills for you.

Glory to God for that sure way – You shall ask what you will and it shall (not might) be done unto you.

Whosoever Shall Say

"For assuredly, I say to you, whoever says to this mountain, Be……" (Mark 11:23)

When Jesus was saying/unfolding this truth, He pointed to whosoever. This is very important to note.

I have come across a number of brethren who disqualify themselves from God's blessings, and actually some are merely victims of those fellows who mix up things. They say because we are this or that, you must take what you hear us say and unfortunately sometimes folks take what they have/give and end up mixed up as they are. You know the Bible is a school of its own whereby everyone is accountable directly.

Know You Can Ask What You Will

Well, woman or man, old or young, been to school or not, poor or rich, as long as can say.

Therefore, all believers are suited to this statement from the mouth of our Lord.

What Ever You Ask

"And whatever things you ask in prayer, believing, you will receive." Matt.21:22

Jesus used this blessed word (whatever) to bring to our awareness the unlimited resources of God.

God owns everything, God created all things, John 1:3, For all things were made by Him and without Him was not anything made that was made.

God's wealth through Jesus Christ is immeasurable. So, when Jesus uses this word (whatever) He is only calling to our attention that we may ask what we need without worrying.

So, all things fall in 'whatever' be it very tiny or very big, cheap or expensive, seen or unseen, etc. Act on whatever as God directs.

What Happens When We Pray And Believe God

A man and his family get their miracle

A certain man in one of our churches in Uganda, gave his life to Jesus Christ, and got born again, according to Romans 10:9, "that if you confess with your mouth the Lord Jesus and believe in your heart that God has raised Him from the dead, you will be saved." Originally, he was part of a religious church where they never put emphasis on the need to get born again. This was a very new and exciting experience for him.

Something else that ignited his being was the teaching of the Word in our church services. He could be seen searching the scriptures as the Word came forth. Like the people of God in Berea, whom the Bible in Acts 17:11-12 states that "these were more fair-minded than those in Thessalonica, in that they received the word with all readiness, and searched the Scriptures daily to find out whether these things were so. Therefore many of them believed, and also not a few of the Greeks, prominent women as well as men. He paid heed to the teaching as by the Holy Spirit I explained to the people through the scriptures, John

Know You Can Ask What You Will

15:7 He was married with six children and lived not very far from the church. After he became born again, he encouraged his wife and children to join him at this new church he had found, and great enough, they did exactly that.

This brother in Christ and his wife didn't have a car and the house they lived in needed a lot of work. Their income was not all that much. However, as they heeded the teachings of the Word of God, their faith grew. One night I was conducting the evening service in Africa, teaching the Word under the anointing, with the power of God present, and people were being healed. "Most assuredly I say to you, he who believes in me, the works that I do he will do also and greater works than these he will do, because I go to my Father, and whatever you ask in my name, that I will do, that the Father may be glorified in the son. If you ask anything in my name, I will do it." John 14:12. It was an atmosphere charged with faith and the people of God were asking and receiving miracles from the Lord God Almighty. Suddenly, this man came forth with a prayer request, right in the midst of the church

What Happens When We Pray And Believe God

Service. He said he had asked the Lord God in the name of Jesus Christ his son to give him a brand new van that seats at least eight people and also had asked for a seven bedroom house with a garage to park his van in. He also asked for some money to purchase a business for his family. I could see faith in his eyes, all he wanted was to come in agreement with him in regards to his prayer request. We gladly did so, for we believe that with God all things are possible. "For with God nothing shall be impossible," according to Luke 1:37.

He went home believing by faith that God Almighty had granted his prayer request and something super natural was to happen to bring about the manifestation of the house, the van and money for business. Remember this book is about what happens when we pray and believe God; this man kept thanking God for His answer to his prayer. Some people out there who know his income ridiculed him and mocked his family even to the point of rebuking him in regard to his faith that God can provide what he had asked for, but he kept believing and learning the Word of God. Now

Know You Can Ask What You Will

it happened that one of his friends of a different faith learned that his former friend in the world had "gotten born again," and it made him very upset because he no longer went out with them to drink alcohol, or listen to music. He had become "somebody else." "Therefore, if anyone is in Christ, he is a new creation, old things have passed away, behold all things have become new." (2 Corinthians 5:17), and this bothered him, he could get on the phone and talk about it to his friends and relatives for he was not understanding what happened to his friend.

One day, a son of this man who was a friend to our brother in Christ, called from Canada, and as they conversed on the telephone, his father suddenly started to tell him about his friend whom he thought had gone beside himself. The son had known his father's friend and when he was still in Africa and he listened with a lot of interest, especially when his father told him that one of the other proofs that he was out of his right mind is this believing that God was giving him a van and a brand new house!! Well, he did not know that his son in Canada had gotten born

What Happens When You Pray And Believe God

again, and he was attending a good Bible teaching church where the Word was taught under the anointing, a church where they believed that God is not a man that he could lie." God is not a man that he should lie, nor a son of man that He should repent. Has He said, and will He not do it or has He spoken and will He not make it good!" Numbers 23:19 For our brother in Christ and his family were just responding to God, who said, "Ask what you will."

The son of this man who was in Canada, quickly asked for the phone number of the friend of his father, and his father told him that this man is just mad, he does not even have a phone. He is very poor. All that he has is Jesus Christ. Surprising to his father, the son offered to buy him a phone and get him connected, so he would be able to talk to him, and that was accomplished. Our brother in Uganda was able to get a phone by the hand of his friend who did not believe in what he believed in. Remember, what God said in Isaiah 55:8-9: "for my thoughts are not your thoughts, nor are your ways my ways, says the Lord. For as the heavens are higher than the earth, so are my ways

Know You Can Ask What You Will

higher than your ways, and my thoughts than your thoughts."

The son of his friend in Canada became very interested in what this man in Africa was talking about and told his story and faith about what he was believing for. They all thought it was great and felt led by God to buy him a brand new van, as well as build him a seven bedroom house, which they did with joy. They also gave him money to start an import business. I saw this miracle taking place. All of us who knew this family in Christ, were rejoicing with them and many of his friends were born again as a result of this answered prayer. Even his friend who thought that this brother in Christ's confession of believing that God can do exceedingly, abundantly beyond what we could think or ask," was a joke, turned around and gave his life to Jesus Christ, and became part of the church.

Beloved, God Almighty is putting together an answer to your prayer, you may not have all the details about it, but He is very able to bring in manifestation what

What Happens When You Pray And Believe God

You have prayed and believed for, from Him. "To him who is able to do exceedingly, abundantly above all that we can ask or think, according to the power that works in us." Ephesians 3:20-21, and go ahead and ask for what you will, and it will be done for you. Don't be shy about it, only believe.

2

FOUNDATIONAL TRUTH II

HAVE FAITH IN GOD

"But without faith it is impossible to please Him, for he who comes to God must believe that He is, and that He is a rewarder of those who diligently seek Him." Heb. 11:6

Your possession of this book right now, is proof that God Almighty is taking you on a journey by the Holy Spirit to cause your faith to emerge strong and mount up with wings like eagles.

The word of God says in Isaiah 40:31, *"But those who wait on the Lord shall renew their strength. They shall mount up with wings like eagles. They shall run and not be weary, they shall walk and not faint."*

It is time for exploits in God, He wants you to possess the land, to be a repairer of places to dwell in, to not only bless you but make you a blessing, so that you may have something to share with others. God believes in you, especially since you received His son. *"What then shall we say to these things, if God is for us, who can be against us? He who did not spare His own son, but delivered him up for us all. How shall He not with Him also freely give us all things?..."* Romans 8:31-38

Remember also what our Lord Jesus Christ said to Nicodemus, concerning salvation, whereby our Lord and savior put emphasis on the necessity of being born again, which you are already. In case you are not born again yet, you need to give your life to Jesus Christ right now and confess Him as your lord and savior as we are flowing more in this revelation of what happens when we pray and believe God. *"Jesus answered and said to him, "Most assuredly, I say to you, unless one is born again, he cannot see the kingdom of God."* John 3:3

How I was filled with the Holy Spirit

In 1984, while a student of Irrigation and Water Conservation at Hahai University in China, Nanjing, I happened also to be studying Theology by correspondence. I was enrolled in a degree program

Have Faith In God

with a university outside China. I was really hungry for the things of God. *"Blessed are those who hunger and thirst for righteousness, for they shall be filled."* Matt. 5:6 and I did ask the Lord to give me every virtue that pertains to godliness. All around me I was surrounded by people who knew little about God. Most of the Chinese students were told that God is not there, and that He does not exist and many had believed it. So, they were on their own, not looking to God for anything. There were no churches in the community teaching the word of God. The only fellowship we had as Christians was in one of our fellow Christian student's dormitory once in a while, where we would gather to pray and read the Bible. I was still younger in the Lord and needed growth. So, I had invested some money in Christian authors around the world, whose books helped me in my Christian growth. Now, it happened that one time I ran into a professor of medicine from the United States of America. He taught at one of Nanjing, China University of Medicine. He was a very nice loving man and a born again Christian. I was visiting with

-33-

What Happens When You Pray And Believe God

one of my friends from Africa who was a medical student at that university. When I met him, he had a book with him entitled, <u>The Holy Spirit</u>. I looked through the book and noticed a lot of helpful and important topics that were addressed. All that the author wrote about had scriptures to back it up. So, I asked the brother in Christ from America to let me take it and read it, and he gladly did. Don't forget that this book is about "What Happens When We Pray and Believe God," and we are dealing with Foundational Truth II, that is: have faith in God.

This is your moment for action, for faith without works is dead. I acted. I got the book that God brought my way and I recognized that God is a rewarder of those who diligently seek Him. I treasured that book that I had borrowed from this professor of medicine. I read it four times from cover to cover. Please, don't let anything tell you that you tell you that you don't need to read book written by anointed authors. I mean authors who explain the Word of God to us with scripture soundness. Remember the eunuch whom Philip met in Acts

Have Faith In God

Chapter 8: *"So Philip ran to him, and heard him reading the prophet Isaiah, and said, "Do you understand what you are reading?" And he said, "How can I, unless someone guides me?" And he asked Philip to come up and sit with him."* Acts 8:30-31

We need the Ministry of the Written Word, and God raises authors to lead you and guide you to your miracle through explaining important truths in the Bible by revelation knowledge, testimonies like this one are brought to your attention to let you know that God is still very active in your life today, causing you to grope for Him that He may show Himself great on your behalf. "So that they should seek the Lord in the hope that they might grope for Him and find Him, though He is not far from each one of us." Acts 17:27

NKJV. It is not just you seeking God, He, himself is Seeking for you. That is one of the reasons this book is in your hands right now. The purpose of this revelation about "What Happens When We Pray and Believe God," is to cause you to arise and shine and reach out for what God has prepared for you already by the Holy Spirit through His son Jesus Christ. *"For the eyes of the Lord run to and fro throughout the*

What Happens When We Pray And Believe God

whole earth to show Himself strong on behalf of those whose heart is royal to Him…" II Chronicles 16:9, and that is you. Seize this moment like I seized mine!

Reading that book, "The Holy Spirit," helped me to understand that it was God's will for me to be filled with the Holy Spirit with evidence of speaking in tongues." *For this is good and acceptable in the sight of God our Savior, who desires all men to be saved and to come to the knowledge of the truth."* 1Timothy 2:3-4 Being an engineering student at Hahai University in China was a very wonderful time of discovery. We had text books that helped us to taste and prove things. There was a lot of mathematics involved as well as science, so I knew how to "search out matters," and that is how I approached things of the Bible.

I had to get proof from the Holy Bible about anything said or written. I had been a Catholic for a long time, until I got born again. A few years before that time and then being a Catholic you were never really introduced to the Bible. We never read it nor took it with us to the Catholic Mass!! But now, thank God I got hold of the Holy Book – the Bible, and I could

Have Faith In God

Find out what God said about me. So I started asking God for the Baptism of the Holy Spirit with evidence of speaking in tongues, like what happened in Acts 10: 44-47, *"While Peter was still speaking these words, the Holy Spirit fell upon all those who heard these word. And those of the circumcision who believed were astonished as many as came with Peter, because the gift of the Holy Spirit had been poured out on the Gentiles also. For they heard them speak with tongues and magnify God. Then Peter answered, "Can anyone forbid water, that these should not be baptized who have received the Holy Spirit just as we have?"* Here Peter based his conclusion on evidence for they heard them speak in tongues.

If you have never been baptized with the Holy Spirit with evidence of speaking in tongues, it's time for you to ask. You may say, "Why is this very important to me? Especially since this book is about "What Happens When We Pray and Believe God." I will tell you why right here, for tongues are part of the language to help you in prayer. *"Praying always with all prayer and supplication in the spirit, being watchful to this end with all perseverance and*

What Happens When We Pray And Believe God

supplication for the Saints..." Ephesians 6:18. The Holy Spirit helps us in our weaknesses as well, *"Likewise the Spirit also helps us in our weaknesses. For we do not know what we should pray for as we ought, but the Holy Spirit Himself makes intercession for us with groanings which cannot be uttered. Now He who searches the hearts knows what the mind of the Spirit is because He makes intercession for the Saints according to the will of God."* Romans 8: 26-27. We need the help of the Holy Spirit in prayer and thank God that help is available to all children of God. "Then Peter said to them, *'Repent, and let every one of you be baptized in the Name of Jesus Christ for the remission of sin; and you shall receive the gift of the Holy Spirit.*

For the promise is to you and to your children and to all who are afar off as many as the Lord our God will call..." Acts 2:38-39. That is me and you. I was in China when I found that truth, I asked and God granted my petition. I received the Baptism of the Holy Spirit, with evidence of speaking in tongues and never remained the same again, apart from getting saved, this second experience of being Baptized in the

Holy Spirit would be the greatest experience in my life in regard to answered prayer. Well, I only wanted to share this interesting testimony with you, as we look at Fundamental Truth II, Having Faith in God.

Having Faith in God

And Jesus answered them, Have faith in God. (Mark 11:22)

As God's word abides in us, our faith in him grows and this is well pleasing to God that we have faith in Him.

Jesus finding no figs on the fig tree said to it, "No man eat fruit of thee hereafter forever," and his disciples heard it. Mark 11:14. Next day as they passed by in the morning, Peter said to Jesus, "Master, behold the fig tree which thou cursed is withered away." And Jesus answered them, "Have faith in God". Mark 11:22

This tree, speaking from the natural point of view, did not wither immediately when Jesus spoke to it. This the disciples had noted. Actually, they didn't know what was going to happen to the tree afterwards. That

What Happens When We Pray And Believe God

is why Peter expresses surprise when the next day they find the tree withered from root to top.

And Jesus answered them by only telling them what we are required to do. Jesus is saying to them – that is the normal; when a man has faith in God.

Maybe they had thought His word had gone void. However, in His word He says, *".....It shall not return to me void, but it shall accomplish that which I please and it shall prosper in the thing where I send it."* (Isaiah 55:11).

Beloved, we need to believe God, then things will be wrought by us.

Bartimaeus Receives His Sight

Mark 10:46 – And they came to Jericho and as he went out of Jericho with his disciples and a great number of people, blind Bartimaeus, the son of Timaeus, sat by the highway side begging. Verse 47 – And when he heard that it was Jesus of Nazareth, he began to cry out and say, "Jesus, thou son of David, have mercy on me." Bartimaeus must have heard about the things Jesus was doing and inquired about his identity.

Have Faith In God

People would talk, for the fame of Jesus had spread all over the place. They would speak some things in the hearing of Bartimaeus, "oh my, a blind man saw when he met Jesus," "a lame man walked when he met Jesus," "a paralyzed man received his healing when brought to Jesus," "a leper was cleansed of leprosy," and so on and so on. Through these testimonies, the faith of Bartimaeus in Christ, increased the more when he heard the news.

Remember, faith comes by hearing, and hearing things of God – the word. To Bartimaeus , Jesus was invisible, for he could only hear him when He spoke, feel him when he was touched, but could not see him for he was blind.

Today, though Jesus in not with us physically, we know he is with us – so our case resembles that of Bartimaeus in a way. Both of us can only reach unto Him by faith. Mark 10:48 – And many charged him that he should hold his peace but he cried the more a great deal. *"Thou son of David, have mercy on me."*

That's it. The kind of help those with Jesus saw fit for Bartimaeus was to charge him to hold his peace – but the man was blind. What peace should he hold? In

What Happens When We Pray And Believe God

things of seeing he had no peace. You say, brother that happened in those days, it is no longer happening. No, never, it is still happening. Folks still charge others to keep their peace and some accept such orders and go along in distress while they could have turned to the Saviour and be restored.

We need not allow circumstances, people, our minds (when not renewed with the word of God), feelings and the devil to charge us to keep quiet when we know it's the will of God for us to do whatever He wants us to do. God requires of us the faith which is not governed by those things but which takes Him at His word.

It seems Bartimaeus was saying to these people, I know who my Redeemer is and He lives."

Mark 10:49 – And Jesus stood still and commanded him to be called, and they called the blind man, saying unto him, "Be of good comfort, rise, he calleth thee.

Now you realize, these folks didn't know much either. The way how they have changed their approach to the whole matter carries a message of this nature. Oh, so it can work! Ah, Bartimaeus you are right! Glory to

Have Faith In God

God!, they learned something thereafter. And casting away his garment, rose and came to Jesus. Mark 10:51 – And Jesus answered and said unto him, "What wilt thou that I should do unto thee?" The blind man said unto him, "Lord, that I might receive my sight." Vs 52 and Jesus said unto him, "go thy way; thy faith hath made thee whole," and immediately he received his sight, and followed Jesus in the way.

What Jesus is saying here is this – All along I had and have all that you need. It is the act of believing for it that has earned it for you and indeed it is your faith that has made you well.

Yes, if it worked for Bartimaeus, it can work for you – your faith.

So, this blind man acted on his faith, he did not allow those people to quiet him down. They even added scolding to help their cause but Bartimaeus stood firm in faith giving glory to God. So beloved, let's believe God without any reservations – in effect giving glory to God. This is your time, this is your moment to glorify God, just reach out to Him and lay hold of what is already yours, which you receive along with

What Happens When We Pray And Believe God

Lazarus Resurrects

Now, a certain man was ill (John 11:1) Lazarus of Bethany, the village of Mary and her sister Martha. Vs2 It was Mary who anointed the Lord with ointment and wiped his feet with her hair, whose brother Lazarus was ill. So the sisters sent to him (Jesus) saying, "Lord, he whom you love is ill."

Vs 5 Now Jesus loved Martha and her sister and Lazarus. V6 So when he heard that he was ill, he stayed two days longer in the place where he was.

KJV (John 11:6) says when he had heard therefore that he was sick, he abode two days still in the same place where he was!

When Mary and Martha sent a message to Jesus, they didn't say, "Please come quickly," they only informed him of the sickness of Lazarus. You say, why? For they were sure he would naturally hurry to the site for they knew Jesus loved Lazarus.

But instead of Jesus doing what normally man expects another man to do when a loved one falls sick, the Bible says the Lord only decided to stay two days

Have Faith In God

longer after getting the message. This is one of the areas where the devil has given people trouble. Know that you are loved of God, that is why He gave his own son to die for you.

Jesus loves you as He loved Mary, Martha and Lazarus. The Word of God says in Col. 2:8-9, *see to it that no one makes a prey of you by philosophy and empty deceit according to human tradition, according to the elemental spirits of the universe, and not according to Christ.* Vs9 For in him the whole fullness of deity/God dwells bodily, Vs10 and you have come to full ness of life in Him who is the head of all rule and authority.

In a way, the message which was delivered to Jesus, was the sisters' prayer for their brother Lazarus, as you and I, we do pray to the Lord.

Our state towards Jesus resembles theirs for they were not with Him bodily, in the same place, but we know He is there – in us, by the Holy Spirit – though we may not be seeing Him physically, so did Martha and Mary, and Jesus did receive their prayer.

What Happens When We Pray And Believe God

Something like this sometimes happens when we pray. Instead of things happening quickly as we would like, it seems as if God didn't hear our prayer and actually the devil gets up and tries to capitalize on this. He says a lot of things to cause you to have hard times as God works on your answer. Child of God, we need to be strong in faith after we pray for the Bible says, when we pray, he heareth. So, do not allow traditions of men, elementary spirits/demons, philosophy of men, and other things to perturb you.

Just stay with God, so that, whatever you have prayed to God about, in it the Son of God may be glorified.

Actually, John 11:4 says: but when Jesus heard it, He said, *"This illness is not unto death; it is for the glory of God, so that the Son of God may be glorified by means of it."* So through faith, things like; trials, temptations, hardships can be turned around into incidences of glorifying God, and that's faith.

In John 11:11 Jesus spoke to His disciples and said, "Our friend Lazarus has fallen asleep, but I go to awaken him out of sleep." You know to God what we

Having Faith In God

call big problems, are just nothing, for He is Almighty. Vs12 The disciples said to him, "Lord if he has fallen asleep, he will recover." Now you notice how they answered – what they were saying is: oh, only that – falling asleep – definitely you can awaken him, and also we can do it – they had the confidence along that line, as many have about similar incidences.

Beloved, faith is not letting God do what you can do, that is in case he fails you do it! No, that is not faith, that is self-confidence. Many times faith is taken to be everything else except what it is. Faith is not a mental assertion. We don't believe with heads! We believe with our hearts, for by the heart man believes unto salvation – and other things of God.

Jesus knew the disciples' thoughts. The way they had looked at it, that is why in Vs16 he told them plainly; for he knew that unless He was very clear, they were going to miss the great blessing of their faith in God increasing as a result of this incidence that had occurred, "Lazarus is dead, and for your sake I am glad that I was not there, so that you may believe…". So, in a way, Jesus wanted them to know the differen--

What Happens When We Pray And Believe God

ce between man and God practically. Vs17 Now when Jesus came, he found that Lazarus had already been in the tomb four days.

Vs20-22 When Martha heard that Jesus was coming, she went and met him while Mary sat in the house. Vs21 Martha said to Jesus, "Lord, if you had been here, my brother would not have died. Vs22 And even now I know that whatever you ask from God, God will give you."

In Vs22, you notice how well Martha said it, but she put what would have been her responsibility on Jesus and failed to realize that Jesus was the Lord – God, for the Father and the Son are one. It was for Martha to ask from Jesus.

Jesus said to her, "Your brother will rise again." Martha said to him, "I know that he will rise again in the resurrection at the last day." Now you realize that Martha had not yet believed Jesus. In a way, we are supposed to believe Him – that is holding onto His word. She had a mental attitude of trust as many people sometimes have. No, God wants us to believe with our hearts.

Vs25 Jesus said to her, "I am the resurrection and the life; he who believes in me, though he die, yet shall he live, and whoever lives and believes in me shall

Having Faith In God

never die. Do you believe this?" You see, he had to ask her to clarify her nature of belief, whether it was mental or of the heart. Beloved, faith is of the heart, not of the head.

She said to Him, "Yes Lord, I believe that you are the Christ, the Son of God, He who is coming into the world." That is a good confession.

Vs37 When Mary came where Jesus was and saw him, she fell at his feet, saying to him, "Lord, if you had been here my brother would not have died." You see, they were so much involved with the past, the problem of Jesus not having been there, instead of getting to the solution – that is, solving the problem. This beloved, you should not do, don't cling onto failures or if's, get to the solution – that is Jesus.

Yes, Jesus wept, but was also troubled in His spirit when He saw Mary and the Jews weeping. What troubled Jesus mostly was the failure of Mary and those who were with her to see Him in His proper picture – that is Christ, the Son of God, God with them to whom nothing is too difficult.

You see, the more God is revealed to you through His word, the more your faith in Him grows. That's why it cometh by hearing and hearing by His word.

What Happens When We Pray And Believe God

John 11:39 – Jesus said, "Take away the stone." Martha the sister of the dead man said to him, "Lord, by this time there will be an odor for he has been dead four days." So, what Martha was saying here is: it's all over, he is gone, never to come back even though you are around. She was occupied with man's ways – saying it is impossible to man – and to God! Child of God, get out of your ways and take to God's ways – that's where great thing happen!

Jesus said to her, *"Didn't I tell you that if you would believe you would see the Glory of God?* Faith brings down the Glory of God – it manifests God.

So, they took away the stone and Jesus prayed in their hearing, on their account. When he had said this, he cried out with a loud voice, "Lazarus, come forth."

Yes, Jesus addressed the dead man as if he was alive and this to man is very strange, we don't address corpses, do we? But through God, it is possible. When God speaks, things understand. Whether from the natural point of view they are dead or alive. So beloved when we speak in the Name of Jesus, our words carry a great weight and meaning. Vs44 – The dead man came out, his hands and feet bound with

Having Faith In God

Bandages, and his face wrapped with a cloth. Jesus said to them, "Unbind him, and let him go." Then many of the Jews which came to Mary, and had seen the things which Jesus did, believed on Him.

Yes, have faith in God and things like this will happen in your life and many who will see them will believe unto Christ and others their faith in God will be increased. According to the Bible, you are a king and a priest, "and has made us kings and priests to His God and Father, to Him be glory and dominion forever and ever. Amen." Revelation 1:6, you have authority given to you by our Lord Jesus Christ. Your position, is a position of leadership, whereby your actions when wrought in God do help many walk in the light, so arise and shine for the glory of the Lord has risen upon you!

This book in your hands is part of the answer to your prayers to God in regard to the Great Commission: "And Jesus came and spoke to them, saying, *"All authority has been given to Me in heaven and on earth. Go therefore and make disciples of all the nations, baptizing them in the name of the Father and of the Son and of the Holy Spirit, teaching them to observe all things that I have commanded you; and lo, I am with you always, even to the end of the age."*

What Happens When We Pray And Believe God

You Have Everlasting Life

He that believes on the Son has everlasting life;...(John 3:36) For God so loved the world that he have His only begotten son that whosoever believeth in Him should not perish but have everlasting life. John 3:16

You see, the son of man is lifted up and what is required of us is to believe on Him and have eternal life.

Glory to God, it is for whosoever. You mean even when that whosoever is in America, Asia, Australia, Europe, etc.? Yes, for the Word of God doesn't say, "whosoever" must be in any particular place for this to work for him. What about one who is blind, lame, sick, short, tall, rich, poor, learned, unlearned, clothed, naked, fat, thin, dumb, leader, etc.? Yes, for the Word of God doesn't depend on such things to work. This is one of the areas where many miss it.

You know, receiving the Son of God is the greatest thing your faith can wrought to you and there and then you receive the power to become a Son of God – everlasting life. We believers have this – everlasting life, we are Children of God, and this is the greatest

Having Faith In God

thing man can achieve – to be a Son of God through believing on Christ.

You mean it is greater than all the riches and honors of this world? Yes, it is. And since you could obtain this eternal life, you can have anything else good from God by praying and believing as you believed for this thing.

Now you have eternal life, go ahead and take all other blessings. I haven't said go and have all other blessings for believers have all the blessings of God in Christ. So what we need to do is to take them. You know these blessings are for us legally – for they were paid for by the precious blood of Jesus.

So when poor, believe God, and get rich, sick, believe God for your healing, weak, believe God for strength, blind, believe God for sight, crooked ways – get them straightened up through believing God. For if you believe as you believed unto the Name of His Son, you will receive whatsoever you ask for in prayer.

Child of God, God is not a man that He should lie, neither the son of man that He should repent; has He said, and shall He not do it? Or hath He spoken and shall He not make it good? (Numbers 23:19) Beloved, God has blessed us in Jesus and no one

What Happens When We Pray And Believe God

can reverse it. Expect a miracle! The Lord God Almighty, right now, is stirring up your heart to reach out beyond the natural so that you do have more resources to meet your needs as well as meet the needs of others. You have to have extra money to sow into the work of God. You are not only receiving your healing, but God is causing His healing power to flow through you, so that someone will be healed through your faith.

Jesus said in John 10:10, *"The thief does not come except to steal, and to kill, and to destroy. I have come that they may have life, and that they may have it more abundantly."* The Lord desires you to have abundance, abundant peace, abundant joy, abundant finances, abundant wisdom, abundant revelation in Him and abundant resources to meet the kingdom's needs. Like building churches, purchasing vehicles for ministry, making sure that the prophets, evangelists, pastors, teachers, and apostles are well cared for so that they may concentrate on the Word and not be distracted because of the lack of resources.

"Then the twelve summoned the multitude of the disciples and said, "It is not desirable that we should leave the word of God and serve tables…" Acts 6:2-3 and in effect they stay anointed in the presence of God

Having Faith In God

One of the great needs we have today, is people whose lives are full of the power and miracles of God. Those who can speak and the devils tremble, those children of God who are drawing out of the rich presence of God, for they can dare to believe what the Bible says about them, for when we believe what the Bible says we are, and we act in line with that belief, then we are in position to do exploits and receive what Jesus already purchased for us through His death on the cross. In effect, great things do happen through our lives for we pray and believe God. *"Now this is the confidence that we have in Him, that if we ask anything according to His will, He hears us. And if we know that He hears us, whatever we ask, we know that we have the petitions that we have asked of Him."*
I John 5:14-15

My experience through preaching in a very large number of churches around the world, has enabled me to literally come face to face with the many challenges that we face as believers. That is why it is very good to receive good teaching of the Word of God. It is very clear that God never said that my people are destroyed for lack of resources, or because the devils are so powerful. No, no, no, the Bible says, *"My people are destroyed for lack of knowledge. Because you have rejected knowledge, I also will reject you*

What Happens When We Pray And Believe God

from being priest for Me; Because you have forgotten the law of your God, I also will forget your children." Hosea 4:6

You must read the Bible!

The Bible is a Holy book, containing a message from the Lord God Almighty to all the people; people in Africa, those in America, all in Russia, Australia, Europe, China and everyone. In the Bible we find the will of God, as well, we get to know who we are, whose we are and the purpose for our being here.

We were made in God's image. We are not just a body. Man is a Spirit, with a soul, living in a body. The Bible says, *"And the Lord God formed man of the dust of the ground, and breathed into his nostrils the breath of life; and man became a living being."* Genesis 2:7

We get the revelation of who we are and who God is from the Bible, by reading it as well as studying the Word of God, and also listening to anointed teachers and preachers of the Word, whom God has put in the Body of Christ. A book like this is a blessing from God to you, to make you stronger, wiser, better and cause your faith to soar, to greater heights in Him.

Having Faith In God

Faith is bigger than money, for sometimes God supplies our needs without the use of money. He has done this so many times in your life, and my life. He has healed us, supernaturally; with no application of money or medicine.

God has put a way for us where it seemed to be no way, He has caused deliverance to happen in our lives without using any natural means; but applying His heavenly power to our situations.

In 1992, I met a medical professor's wife in Kampala. This lady could not sleep at night, and she had to take a lot of pills to enable her to have a little bit of sleep. They had tried all that they knew to help her get well, but nothing worked. It was not until they referred her to come to me for prayer.

When I started praying for her, suddenly demons manifested in her life, and I had to take authority over them in the Name of Jesus. Sure enough, we cast them out of the woman, and from that day she was able to sleep again at night, and she did not need the pills prescribed by the doctor, any more. Her husband was amazed, he just could not believe; God did it.

ELOHIM

KATONDA

GOD

3

FOUNDATIONAL TRUTH III

GOD WANTS TO SHOW HIMSELF GREAT ON YOUR BEHALF

"For the eyes of the Lord run to and from throughout the whole earth to show Himself strong on behalf of those whose heart is royal to Him...." 2 Chronicles 16:9

Very beloved of God, one of the most important facts you need to know is this: the idea of prayer originated from God Almighty. It is Him who initiated this amazing process throughout the Bible in various places God invites His people to pray, *"Call upon me and I will answer you, and show you great and mighty things, which you do not know."* Jeremiah 33:3

This book is in your hands today because you called upon Him. God wants your faith in Him to increase, so that when He speaks to you about something He wants to do for you, which is beyond your natural means that you would dare believe Him, knowing that amazing things happen when we pray and believe God. *"Behold, I am the Lord, the God of all flesh. Is there anything too hard for me?"* Jeremiah 32:27

God Miraculously Funds My Trip

In 1998, I received an invitation to attend the ICBM, International Charismatic Bible Ministries at Oral Roberts University, in the U.S.A., Tulsa, Oklahoma. At that time, I was pastoring a church in Kamwokya, Kampala, Uganda, known as Christian Faith Center.

Though People were getting born again and many miracles were taking place among us, and it was "like heaven on earth," we did not have enough money coming in to sponsor my trip to that wonderful conference. I tried to contact some churches to help me with my trip to the U.S.A., but I received no sponsorship. So, what I did with the congregation was to ask God for provision of the round trip plane ticket, money to help me on my trip, money for a place to stay, and a Visa to the United States of America, for Jesus said, *"Ask, and it will be given to you; seek, and you will find; knock, and it will be opened to you. For everyone who asks receives, and he who seeks finds, and to him who knocks it will be opened."* Matt 7:7

God wants to show Himself great on your behalf.

I want to remind you that we are dealing with Foundational Truth III, in regard to What Happens When We Pray and Believe God, for you to get the most out of this revelation concerning calling upon God through prayer. I want you to understand that I did not have even a dollar bill in my account towards this trip.

I was busy, faithfully ministering to God's people and they would give tithes and offerings in the daily services, but there was no surplus from the church offerings available to help me with this trip.

During this time, all I had to do was to completely look to God for divine provision. I needed at least $3,000.00 in order to make this trip.

You might be wanting to do something for someone or for yourself, but for right now, it seems like all the finances you have, have been allocated to something else; bills, and it looks as if you can't go another extra mile to do greater works. I do have great news for you, just keep on reading, and expect God to show Himself great on your behalf, like He did for me in this case.

There was a deadline for the visa application from the

What Happens When We Pray and Believe God

American Embassy, and also the time to be on the flight, for the dates of the ICBN Conference at Oral Roberts University in Tulsa, Oklahoma were definite and already set. Now, it happened as I was preaching in another church, a full-gospel church, God had led me to pray for three gentlemen about their businesses, and that was quite some time ago. The Lord had given me a Word of Knowledge that there were three gentlemen whose businesses were going through severe and trying times, whereby it would take an act of God to turn their situations around.

Surely, the three men stepped out and when they raised their hands up, the power of God fell on them in an amazing way. The presence of God was so strong on them until they could not stand on their feet, because of God's Glory.

God blessed them and miraculously turned their lives around. Right there, they received their joy back! The sadness due to the losses they previously had encountered when conducting business, completely left. There and then they gave glory to God.

It was like what happened in Samaria, "Then Philip went down to the city of Samaria and preached Christ to them. And the multitudes with one accord heeded

God wants to show Himself great on your behalf

The things spoken by Philip hearing and seeing the miracles which he did. For unclean spirits, crying with a loud voice, came out of many who were possessed; and many who were paralyzed and lame were healed. *And there was great joy in the city."* Acts 8:5-8.

I had preached Christ Jesus that day, I preached and taught about the awesomeness of God, and that God is Almighty.

The entire atmosphere was charged with God's tangible power, and spirits of unbelief had vacated the premises. One could see faith in the eyes of the people of God; they were ready for great exploits.

So, it happened, as I was traveling through Kampala, the capital city of Uganda, in Africa, walking down on William Street, when suddenly I heard someone calling me saying, "Pastor, Pastor, Pastor Kayiwa, it's me, your brother in Christ, do you remember me?" So I stopped and looked behind me, to figure out who was reaching out to me.

It seems that I had passed him standing by one of the shops, and I had not recognized him at that time. He then came to me and said, "Please come to my office.

What Happens When We Pray and Believe God

I would like to talk to you." However, I told him that I was on my way to the American Embassy, to try to ask them to give me an extension for payment of the money required to obtain a Visa to the U.S.A. I did not have the money at that time, and did not want them to deny me the Visa for such an important trip I needed to take.

However, he insisted that I go to his office with him, for he wanted to tell me about the miracle God did for him, when I prayed for him in church. Well, I followed him to his office and interestingly enough, he asked me about this trip I was working on to visit the U.S.A., what it meant, and immediately on finding out what God had put in my heart to believe for, he called his wife and informed her that he felt he had a leading for the two of them to pay for my Visa to the U.S.A., right away.

He said, "This man of God prayed for us and our business is booming. We need to bless him." So, he immediately pulled out his car and drove me to the embassy, where he went ahead and paid for my Visa. On the way, he told me how God turned around his business and caused it to move into prosperity. That now, all of his family and the people he serves through

God wants to show Himself great on your behalf

the work of his hands; he and his wife are experiencing the financial blessing from the Lord.

He drove me back to the church that I pastored, with joy, and I was so glad to see God using him, for me to get a visa to the U.S.A.

I have a prophetic word for you. The Lord says, *"Believe Him, know that He is Almighty, and go forth trusting Him with all your heart, for now He is doing something new in your life – showing Himself great on your behalf, and be not anxious for the Lord is fully in charge of the whole matter,"* says the Lord God Almighty.

As you are well aware, I obtained the American Visa, a very important aspect to my journey, and now all I needed was the airplane ticket. I continued to trust God, *"Trust in the Lord with all your heart. Lean not on your own understanding; in all thy ways acknowledge Him, and He shall direct your path.* Proverbs 3:5-6.

The manifestation of the money for my visa supernaturally was a big boost to my faith. I was able to experience a bit of what happens when we pray

What Happens When We Pray And Believe God

and believe God, and I knew in my heart that God was able, "being confident of this very thing that He who has been a good work in will complete it until the day of Jesus Christ." Philippians 1:6 For I was not even remembering that man nor looking out for him. I was just taking care of the Lord's business when suddenly I ran into him - nothing less than a miracle!!

This precious brother in Christ told me, that when I get a ticket, he would be more than happy to drive me to the airport. Well, that let me know that he did not have a plane ticket for me!!! He had been used by God to provide a visa!

I had already gone ahead and booked the round trip flight to the U.S.A. in faith, and they had my reservation. What the ticket office was waiting for was my payment, money.

The day came on which I was supposed to be on the plane, but, I still, in the natural, did not have the plane ticket. I got ready that morning, and as I was preparing to leave, the gentleman who promised to take me to the airport came to get met and said that a certain man who owed him $100, out of the blue called this morning and asked him to pick the money

God Wants to Show Himself Great on Your Behalf

from his house. So he went by and picked it up on his way to my place, to take me to the airport. At that time, a round trip ticket to the U.S.A. was over $1,800.00 and I had not gotten that money yet, but part of the cost included a one-way ticket from Entebbe to Nairobi, Kenya that was around $90.

I thanked the man for $100. He didn't even know that I did not yet have the plane ticket. So, he drove me to the airport, and when arrived at the Entebbe International Airport, in Uganda, Africa, I then asked him to watch my belongings for a few minutes as I went to talk to the people at the ticketing office. The Lord had witnessed in my spirit that I was going to fly out of Uganda that day. It was an inner witness.

I knew that I knew I would be on a flight out of the country that afternoon, for the Spirit of God was bearing witness to my spirit that it was so. *"For as many as are led by the Spirit of God, these are sons of God. For you did not receive spirit of bondage again to fear, but you received the Spirit of adoption by whom we cry out "Abba, Father."* The Spirit Himself bears witness with our spirit that we are children of God." Romans 8:14-15. The same way you know that you know that you are a child of God; is the same way the Holy Spirit bears witness with our spirits when

What Happens When We Pray And Believe God

God is ordering our steps. *"Trust the Lord with all your heart, and lean not on your own understanding; in all your ways acknowledge Him and He shall direct your path."* Proverbs 3:5

God does direct your path. He is able to order your steps from within. Do expect a miracle and know that there is nothing too hard for the Lord. "Is anything too hard for the Lord?..." Genesis 18:14.

Now, at the ticket office, I was able to get a one-way plane ticket to Nairobi, Kenya, Africa, for less than $100. I waved goodbye to my friend, and got on the plane. The flight took less than two hours. During the flight, I was just astonished at how God was working everything out on this trip to the U.S.A., and I continued praising and worshipping God in my heart throughout the journey.

Beloved of God, you and I are on this trip in this book, of having a glimpse of what happens when we pray and believe God. We are dealing with Foundational Truth III. God Wants to Show Himself Great on Your Behalf with the Understanding that God is preparing you for exploits; and it is happening now; right now in your life. You are reading this book by divine providence. You love God and you seek after Him,

God Wants to Show Himself Great on Your Behalf

"Those who do wickedly against the covenant, he shall corrupt with flattery; but the people who know their God shall be strong and carry out great exploits." Daniel 11:32 Let the Lord lead you, like I let him help me to get on my trip to the U.S.A. without the plane ticket.

Now, when I arrived at Kenyatta Airport, Nairobi, I went to the office of the airline that does ticketing to find out if anyone, somewhere, had paid for my round trip ticket to the U.SA., only to be informed that I did not have any ticket paid for. So I continued praying in the Spirit within my heart, for I needed to stay edified. *"He who speaks in a tongue edifies himself..."* I Corinthians 14:4 I had to make sure that I stay in the presence of God, for this was like walking on water.

I slept in a seat at the airport that night, but as it was dawning and the sun was about to come out, a very interesting idea come into my heart. I suddenly remembered, a brother in Christ I had prayed for in the Name of Jesus Christ, and saw a miracle of God's provision, for his family. I had told him by the leading of the Holy Spirit, through the Word of Wisdom, that he would get a very good paying job within seven

What Happens When We Pray And Believe God

days, which had appeared as the Lord showed me. God brought these to my remembrance, "But the Helper, the Holy Spirit, whom the Father will send in my name, He will teach you all things, and bring to your remembrance all things that I said to you." John 14:26. Though I had not contacted nor talked to this wonderful child of God for nearly three years. I felt like God was leading me to find him.

He had gotten a promotion within coffee marketing Board of Regents and was now working at the office in Dar es Salaam as there Chief Accountant. I didn't have all the details but at least I knew that he and his wife and children were in Dar es Salam, Tanzania, Africa. This gentleman loved God and really trusted in Him. I had known him as a person who could dare pray and believe God. The job he had gotten was through a supernatural act of God and he knew it also. He was their accountant.

This revelation about him was so real; it was God leading me. I knew that I knew, that I knew I was supposed to be on my way to Dar es Salaam, Tanzania, Africa. "For the Word of God is living and powerful, and sharper than any two-edged sword, piercing even to the division of soul and spirit and of

God Wants to Show Himself Great on Your Behalf

joints and marrow, and is a discerner of the thoughts of and intents of the heart,..." Hebrews 4:12-13. Wherefore, I left the airport and went and booked a bus ticket to Dar es Salaam, for that was where I believed this brother was staying.

I didn't have his phone number nor had I been in Tanzania before. I was venturing into something new, just trusting God, so I got on the bus and arrived in Tanzania in the evening on the next day.

Tanzania is a beautiful nation with wonderful people, and when I got off the bus, I met nice people who seemed pleased to meet a preacher from Uganda. Especially due to the fact that many had to take arms to liberate Uganda from the dictator, Idi Amin and his evil henchmen who had caused a lot of suffering to the people of Uganda and Tanzania.

Some of the people at the bus station asked, "Pastor, are you going to preach in Dar es Salaam?" I told them that whatever the Lord God desires will be done, for "The steps of a good man are ordered by the Lord, and He delights in his way." Psalms 37:23

Remember when you received Jesus Christ as your personal Savior. You became a delight of God for you

What Happens When We Pray And Believe God

are a new creation. Jesus became your righteousness and God does order your steps.

I inquired about the whereabouts of the Ugandan Coffee Marketing Board Depot in Dar es Salaam and they were able to inform me of how to get there; and I arrived at those offices in time, before they left for the day.

When my brother in Christ heard that I was at the main gate, immediately he came to meet me, full of joy. He introduced me to all of his fellow workers, saying, "This is the man of God who prayed with me for me to get this job." I mean the whole place was filled with joy! He told them, "If you need any kind of miracle, you ask him to pray for you and you will see – *God showing Himself great on your behalf*!!"

Well, I stayed in Dar es Salaam one full month, preaching at an Assemblies of God Church every Sunday and some week days.

God healed the people in Tanzania of various ailments such as high blood pressure, cancer, AIDS, pneumonia, tuberculosis, back pains, blood disorders, arthritis and many other ailments. I also performed weddings. It was a glorious moment and a number of

God Wants to Show Himself Great on Your Behalf

people were born again and received the Baptism of the Holy Spirit with evidence of speaking in tongues.

The pastor of the church was a wonderful man of God; he really loved God and the people; he gave me an opportunity to minister and be a blessing to the nation of Tanzania.

All that time, I stayed with my brother in Christ from Uganda and his family, I did not need to worry about what to eat or drink. *"Therefore do not worry, saying, 'What shall we eat?' or 'What shall we drink?' or 'What shall we wear?' For after all these things the Gentiles seek. For your heavenly father knows that you need all these things." But seek first the kingdom of God and His righteousness, and all these things shall be added to you."* Matthew 6:31-33

He spoke to the staff at his place of work that, "Bishop Leonard Kayiwa, his guest and our brother in Christ, was on his way to the U.S.A., but he needed a round trip ticket, as well as money to use while there." Upon hearing that, they quickly reached into their pockets and came up with the money for my ticket, as well as pocket money that would help me on my journey.

Beloved, I flew out of Tanzania miraculously, and God supplied all of my needs according to His riches

What Happens When We Pray and Believe God

in Christ Jesus. "Be anxious for nothing, but in everything by prayer and supplication, with thanksgiving, let your requests be made known to God; and the peace of God which surpasses all understanding will guard your hearts and minds through Christ Jesus." Philippians 4:6, and I also had that peace which surpasses understanding.

This is the prophetic word for you right now! "Arise and shine, reach out beyond the natural, for God is calling you to greater heights, exploits and those inner witnesses you have from the Lord, concerning the nice things He is doing and about to do through your life. You shall see and experience, for the Lord God is with you and "I shall not let any of my words concerning your life fall to the ground. And in this season, I make it good for you," says the Lord.

That God Is

But without faith it is impossible to please him; for he that cometh to God must believe that he is, and that he is a rewarder of them that diligently seek him (Heb. 11:6)

There is a lot of meaning in this statement. You can sing, preach while in some practical situation you indirectly do not affirm this – that He is.

God Wants to Show Himself Great on Your Behalf

You say, how can that be? Yes, it is possible. When trials, temptations and other things come our way, and in such hard circumstances behave as it God is not. We need always, be it what circumstance, to affirm that God is, through a faith that worships Him – in effect pleasing Him. When it is affirmed that God is in control, even when circumstances change, seemingly to worse, we stay steadily holding on Him by a faith that worships; affirming that He is.

VOICE OF FAITH

"…..and by it (faith) he (Abel) being dead yet speaketh:" Hebrews 11:4. Faith speaks, faith has a voice, and it can shout down all other voices – voices of doubt and its voice can be heard in heaven for it is a voice of worship.

Faith says, though in the natural water does not turn into wine, but because through whom all things were made and none (existed) was without Him, has said it, go ahead fill the jars, *"Jesus said to them, "Fill the water pots with water." And they filled them up to the brim."* John 2:7-8 and serve it. - That is worship practically.

We should affirm that God is, by the kind of faith that

What Happens When We Pray And Believe God

holds on God's word, whether people, circumstances, our thought, the devil, etc., all say no. In effect affirming that God created all things and by His will they were given (existence) life and they are totally at His command He can do whatever He wants to do, any time He wants to do it and nothing can stop His word from prospering– and definitely, that's a voice of faith – that's worship.

Faith says, even if the fig tree has no fruit and no grapes grow on the vines, even if the sheep all die and cattle stalls are empty, I will still be joyful and glad because the sovereign God – one existing as an answer to any problem He is, and empowers me divinely – that's worship. *"Though the fig tree may not blossom, Nor fruit be on the vines; Though the flock may be cut off from the fold, And there be no herd in the stalls – Yet I will rejoice in the Lord, I will joy in the God of my salvation. The Lord God is my strength; He will make my feet like deer's feet, And He will make my feet like deer's feet, And He will make me walk on my high hills."* Habakkuk 3:17-19.

Believe That Ye Receive Them

Mark 11:24 – *Therefore I say unto you, what things*

God Wants to Show Himself Great on Your Behalf

so ever ye desire, when ye pray believe that ye receive them. Mark 11:24

In this verse, Jesus is instructing us to believe that we receive – that is your part to play. This is another place where many have missed it. Thanks to God, we have the Word of God. John 8:32 says, "And you shall know the truth and the truth shall make you free."

How you receive – that is God's side, as long as you do your part, God is faithful, He will do His part. His name is the Lord Almighty, to whom nothing is too difficult.

Many wonder how it works. They say, yes, it is true, you have to believe that you receive, But…And they add all kinds of things and they end up mixed up. One asked me, "What if one believes God and sits there?" May be you are asking the same question. Okay, let's search in the word for an answer.

You know, normally, in the natural, we need to have certain things, in order to get other things, things like wisdom, strength, health, people and many others and I want you to note that to God, as a creator, all these are things, and God can provide all these things when

What Happens When We Pray And Believe God

necessary – He really does it and does it wonderfully.

Solomon prayed, 1 Kings 3:9 – "Give, therefore, thy servant an understanding heart to judge thy people, that I may discern between good and bad...vs 11- God answered, Behold, I have done according to thy words; Lo I have given thee a wise and an understanding heart;...

God has wisdom and if it requires wisdom for you to receive whatever you asked for, He will impart wisdom on you, and you will then clearly see the way to receive it.

"And the Spirit of the Lord came mightily upon him." Another translation says, suddenly the power of the Lord made Samson strong and he rent him (the lion) as he would have rent a kid, and he had nothing in his hand...Judges 14:6

God has power. Through His Spirit He can make you strong. So, if it requires strength and power for you to receive, He will provide that.

And the Word of the Lord came unto him (Elijah) saying, "Get thee hence and turn thee eastward and hide thyself by the brook Cherith that is before Jordan.

God Wants to Show Himself Great on Your Behalf

And the word of the Lord came unto him (Elijah) saying, Get thee hence and turn thee eastward and hide thyself by the brook Cherith that is before Jordan. And it shall be that thou shalt drink of the brook and I have commanded the raven to feed thee there. (I Kings 17:3-4). So he went and did according to the word of the Lord; for he went and dwelt by the brook Cherith, that is before Jordan and the raven brought him bread and flesh in the morning and bread and flesh in the evening; and he drank of the brook.

So if it requires you to be served by birds, people, animals, etc., God will command, and it shall be done.

And Elisha said unto her, "What shall I do for thee? Tell me, what hast though in the house?" And she said, "Thine handmaid hath not anything in the house, save a pot of oil. Then he said, *"Go borrow thee vessels abroad of all thy neighbors, even empty vessels; borrow not a few. And thou shalt shut the door upon thee and upon thy sons, and shalt pour out into all those vessels, and thou shalt set aside that which is full...."*

And it came to pass, when the vessels were full, that she said unto her sons, "Bring me yet a vessel." And they said unto her, "There is not a vessel more." And

What Happens When We Pray and Believe God

oil stopped. Then she came and told the man of God. And he said, go, and sell the oil, and pay thy debt and live thou and thy sons of the rest.

So, if it requires something like this for you to receive what you are believing for, God will do it.

Judges 7:21 – Every man stood in his place round the camp, and the whole enemy ran away yelling while Gideon's men were blowing their trumpets. The Lord mad the enemy troops attack each other with their swords. They ran towards Zarethan as far… So if it requires something like this to happen for you to receive your answer, God will cause it to happen.

Judges 15:18 – Then Samson became very thirsty. So he called to the Lord and said, "You gave me this great victory; am I now going to die of thirst. So he called to the Lord and said, *"You gave me this great victory; am I now going to die of thirst and be captured by these heathen Philistines?"* vs 19 Then God opened a hollow place in the ground there at Lehi, and water came out of it. Samson drank it and began to feel much better. So the spring…, if for you to receive the answer, something like this needs to be done, God will do it. Right now the Lord God Almighty is doing a miracle for you. Expect a real turnaround in your life.

God Want to Show Himself Great on Your Behalf

I Sam. 6:9 – Then watch it go; if it goes towards the town of Bethshemesh, this means that it is the God of the Israelite who has sent this terrible disaster on us. But if it doesn't, then we will know that he did not send the plague; it was only of chance.

And they laid the ark of the Lord upon the cart and the coffer with the mice of gold and the images of their emerods. And the kine took the straight way to the way of Bethshemesh, and went along the highway, lowing as they went, and turned not aside to the right hand or to the left; and the lords of the Philistines went after them unto the border of Bethshemesh. So God's hand was in it guiding the kine. So if it requires something like this for you to receive your answer, God will do it.

Luke 4:29 – They rose up, dragged Jesus out of the town and took him to the top of the hill on which their town was built. They meant to throw him over the cliff, but he walked through the middle of the crowd and went his way. So if it requires God to change the intentions of some people as you receive the answer to your prayer of faith, God will do that.

Dan. 3:22 – Now the king had given strict orders for the furnace to be made extremely hot.

What Happens When We Pray and Believe God

The flames even burnt up the guards who took the men to the furnace.

Then Shadrach, Meshack and Abednego, still tied up, fell into the heart of the blazing fire.

Suddenly, Nebuchadnezzar leapt to his feet in amazement. He asked his officials, "Didn't we tie up three men and throw them into the blazing furnace?" They answered, "Yes we did your majesty." *"Then why do I see four men walking about in the fire?"* he asked. "They are not tied up and they show no sign of being hurt – and the fourth one looks like an angel…Vs27 Their hair was not singled, their clothes were not burnt, and there was no smell of smoke on them. If it requires something like this as an answer to prayer, God will do it.

What Is Impossible For Man IS Possible For God (Matt. 19:26)

Num. 11:21 – Moses said to the Lord, "Here I am leading 600,000 people and you say that you will give them enough meat for a month! Could enough cattle and sheep be killed to satisfy them? Are all the fish in the sea enough for them?"

And this is the nature of questions which many have, and sometimes cling to and fail to please God. We

God Wants to Show Himself Great on Your Behalf

should be most concerned with our part – that's believing – the other side of provision is God's, for to him there is no limit to his power.

Num. 11:23 – And the Lord said unto Moses, "Is the Lord's hand waxed short? Thou shalt see now whether my word shall come to pass unto thee or not…"

Vs 31 And there went forth a wind from the Lord and brought quails from the sea, and let them fall by the camp as it were a day's journey on this side, as it were a day's journey on the other side around about the camp, and as it were two cubits high upon the face of the earth.

There is no limit to God's power. We only need to do our part and he does his. God has infinite ways of causing things to happen. So, in this case he used the wind.

You must quit going by feelings, sight and thoughts and get to tapping that unlimited power of God through faith, a faith that worships God, a faith that lets God take over – believing you received it when you haven't yet touched it – taking God at his word. This is what God demands of us.

What Happens When We Pray and Believe God

Exodus 3:21 – I will make the Egyptians respect you so that when my people leave, they will not go empty-handed. So how he does it, that's up to God. What here Moses was required of is to do what the Lord told him. And actually, God caused it to happen. In this case God was telling Moses of what he was going to do, as Moses does the part he has instructed him to do.

But Moses said, "No, Lord, don't send me. I have never been a good speaker and I have not become one since you began to speak to me. I am a poor speaker, slow and hesitant." That's how many talk. Don't talk to God like this for God is the answer. You should believe and say as this, "Master" Simon answered, "We worked hard all night long and caught nothing, but if you say so, I will let down the nets." Yes, that's what believing is about; to let God take control – standing still in a way and letting God lead. And I call it getting to the plane of faith, where great things happen.

God's answer is always similar to this, "Who gives man a mouth? Who makes him deaf or dumb? Who gives him sight or makes him blind? It is I, the Lord. Exodus 4:11 Stop doubting and believe God Almighty is showing Himself great on your behalf right now.

God Wants to Show Himself Great on Your Behalf

The heart of a king is in God's hands. He turns it any way He wants. I am talking to you now prophetically, for the Lord is instructing me to strengthen you for great works.

God Almighty is showing Himself great on your behalf now, even as you are reading this book, for through revelation knowledge, you are being enabled to see behind the veil, and this seeing and experience you are going through right now is literally causing your faith to sky rocket. Jesus is saying to you, what He said to him, *"If you can believe, all things are possible to him who believes."* Mark 9:23

You are a chosen generation, a royal priesthood, a Holy nation, a peculiar person, a king and a priest, a new creation, an ambassador of Christ Jesus.

God has given you authority over nations, kingdoms, over demons and all the powers of the enemy, and has also put His word in your mouth: *"...Behold I have put my words in your mouth. See, I have this day set you over the nations and over the kingdoms, To root out and to pull down, To destroy and to throw down, To build and to plant."* Jeremiah 1:9-10

EL-OLAM

EVER-LASTING GOD

4

FOUNDATIONAL TRUTH IV

AS THIS HAPPENS WHEN WE PRAY AND BELIEVE GOD

"Trust in the Lord with all your heart, And lean not on your own understanding; In all your ways acknowledge Him, And He shall direct your paths."
Proverbs 3:5-6

I Samuel 9 – There was a wealthy and influential man named Kish, from the tribe of Benjamin. Vs2 – He had a son named Saul. Some donkeys belonging to Kish had wandered off; so he said to Saul, *"Take one of the servants with you and go and look for the donkeys."* They went through a number of regions but still they did not find them. Vs5 – When they came into the region of Zuph, Saul said to his servant, *"Let's go back home or my father might stop thinking about the donkeys and start worrying about us."* Vs6 – The servant answered, "Wait, in this town there is a holy man who is highly respected because everything he says comes true. Let's go to him, and maybe he can tell us where we can find the donkeys." So here

What Happens When We Pray and Believe God

note Saul's suggestion of going back home and the servant's reply – (chosen of the servants) of seeing the man of God who was in that town!

Vs7 – "If we go to him, what can we give him?" Saul asked. "There is no food left in our packs and we haven't anything to give him, have we?"

Vs8 – The servant answered, *"I have a small silver coin. I can give him that and then he will tell us where we can find them."* You notice the persistence of the servant on this matter!

Vs9-11 – Saul replied, *"A good idea! Let us go."* So they went to the town where the holy man lived and met girls who directed them saying, "In fact, he is just ahead of you. If you hasty, you will catch up with him. As soon as you go into the town, you will find him. He arrived in town today because the people are going to offer a sacrifice on the hill. Vs14 – So Saul and his servant went on to the town and as they were going in they saw Samuel coming out towards them on his way to the place of worship.

Now I want you to note this carefully. Vs15 – Now on the previous day the Lord had said to Samuel, *"Tomorrow about this time I will send you a man from the tribe of Benjamin, anoint him as ruler of my people Israel; and he will rescue them from the Phili-*

As This Happens When We Pray and Believe God

stines. I have seen the suffering of my people and have heard their cries for help."

When Samuel caught sight of Saul, the Lord said to him, "This is the man I told you about. He will rule my people."

Saul left home looking for donkeys, and the suggestion of looking for the seer was from the servant, but, when God spoke to Samuel said, "Tomorrow about this time I will send you…," And has confirmed to Samuel that Saul is the man he has sent. *"My thoughts" says the Lord, "are not like yours and my ways are different from yours. As high as the heavens are above the earth, so high are my ways and thoughts above yours."* So it was God that put the idea in the servant's heart.

There we are. We must endeavor to learn God's ways through His word.

Now, we continue. "Then Saul went over to Samuel, who was near the gate and asked, "Tell me, where does the seer live?"

You see, Saul did not even know Samuel. Vs19 – Samuel answered, "I am the seer. Go ahead of me to the place of worship. Both of you are to eat with me today. Tomorrow morning I will answer all your que-

What Happens When We Pray and Believe God

stions and send you on your way. Vs20 – As for the donkeys that were lost three days ago, don't worry about them, they have already been found. So you see the method God used to get Saul to Samuel is no man's way.

Vs22 – Then Samuel led Saul and his servant into the large room and gave them a place at the head of the table where the guests, about thirty in all, were seated.

Samuel said to the cooks, "Bring the piece of meat I gave you, which I told you to set aside." So the cook brought the choice piece of the thigh and placed it before Saul. Samuel said, *"Look, here is the piece that was kept for you. Eat it. I saved it for you to east at this time with the people invited."* So Saul ate with Samuel that day. You need to realize that though Samuel didn't know how God was going to fulfill his word, but all the same, believed and kept a piece of choice meat for Saul.

"My word is like the snow and the rain that come down from the sky to water the earth. They make crops grow and provide seed for sowing and food to eat."

"So also will be the word that I speak – it will not fail to do what I plan for it. It will do everything I send it to do.

As This Happens When We Pray and Believe God

We should believe the word of God as Samuel believed and put the choice piece aside. So when we pray and believe we receive it. God moves in ways which sometimes man can't understand.

Thank God, what we want is the answer. You just believe, if God wants to use your hands or feet He will do that, if He wants to somebody else, He will do it, if He want the answer to spring from nowhere as manna fell from heaven He will do that – for He is God and there is no one like Him, and changes not.

2 Samuel 15:36 – When David was told that Ahithophel had joined Absalom's rebellion, he prayed, *"Please Lord, turn Ahithophel's advice into nonsense."*

When David reached the top of the hill where there was a place of worship, his trusted friend Hushai, the Archite, met him with his clothes torn and with earth on his head. Vs33 – David said to him, "You will be of no help to me if you come with me, Vs44 – but you can help me by returning to the city and telling Absalom that you will now serve him as faithfully as you served his father. And do all you can to oppose any advice that Ahithophel gives.

Vs37 – So Hushai, David's friend, returned to the city just as Absalom was arriving.

What Happens When We Pray and Believe God

I want you to follow this story of the Bible closely. David prayed, and God is working on the answer. We note David's meeting of his trusted friend Hushai. This in a way is similar to when Aaron was coming to meet Moses the time God was instructing him. You need to see God's hand in this.

The Bible says in Exodus 4:27 – *"Meanwhile the Lord had said to Aaron, "Go into the desert to meet Moses."* Hushai's meeting David is partly God working on the answer for David - God sent him.

When David met Hushai he had a word of wisdom from God. God gave him what to say and when he said it, Hushai accepted it, and accepted to act like a traitor by going to Absalom. To do this, he needed special courage or else it was a fateful deed, but he did not fear, he went – for God had provided the strength – for God is working out an answer to the prayer of David.

2 Samuel 16:16 – When Hushai, David's trusted friend, met Absalom, he shouted, "Long live the king! Long live the king!" This is wisdom from above.

"What has happened to your loyalty to your friend David?" Absalom asked him. *"Why didn't you go with him?"* Hushai answered, "How could I! I am on the side of the one chosen by the Lord, by these

As This Happens When We Pray and Believe God

people and by all the Israelites. I will stay with you. After all, whom should I serve if not my master's son? As I served your father, so now I will serve you." Absalom accepted his words and if it was not God in this – working on the answer to the prayer, Absalom might have reacted unfavorably toward Hushai; (Suspected Hushai).

Ahithophel had now started advising Absalom and any advice that Ahithophel gave in those days was accepted as though it were the very words of God: both David and Absalom followed it. So, he used to utter a good counsel.

2 Samuel 17:1 – Not long after that, Ahithophel said to Absalom, *"Let me choose twelve thousand men and tonight, set out after David… I will kill only the king… The rest of the people will be safe."* This seemed like good advice to Absalom and all the Israelite leaders.

However, Absalom said, "Now call Hushai and let us hear what he has to say." And Hushai rejected Ahithophel's advice by calling it no good to the king. God is continuing to carry on the work on behalf of David's prayer. Here, *God moves the king to ask advice from Hushai and Hushai gives a fateful counsel,* and it was taken as being better than Ahithophel's.

What Happens When We Pray and Believe God

In verse 14 the word of the Lord clearly says, the Lord had decided that Ahithophel's good advice would not be followed so that disaster would come on Absalom. So, this confirms that all along, God's hand was in all this, working an answer to David's prayer.

Ahithophel did not wait for the outcome of the hanging advice from Hushai. He went and hanged himself – *for God had blinded the king and elders so that they could not see through Hushai's counsel*, and all ended up working together for the good of David. Finally, Absalom was killed and David was restored to the throne.

God can't fail. It's you who needs to fulfill your part – believe you receive it – and the other side of you shall have it; is God's side. For God says, "I am God and always will be. No one can escape from my power; no one can change what I do."

Sometimes, God does things like this when we pray and believe Him.:

I Kings 17:8 – Then the word of the Lord came to him. Vs9 – Arise, go to Zarephath, which belongs to Sidon and dwell there. Behold, I have commanded a widow there to feed you." Vs10 – So he arose and went to Zarephath; and when he came to the gate of the city, behold, a widow was there gathering sticks.

As This Happens When We Pray and Believe God

The word of God does not say that Elijah went into the town asking or looking for the widow that God had commanded to serve him. It says, he only came to the gate.

The woman was not looking for Elijah. She had come to collect fire sticks, and amazing enough, she was a widow.

Elijah called to her and said, "Bring me a little water in a vessel that I may drink."

And as she was going to bring it, he called to her and said, "Bring me a morsel of bread in your hand." And she said, *"As the Lord your God lives, I have nothing baked, only a handful of meal in a jar and a little oil in a cruse and now I am gathering a couple of sticks that I may go in and prepare it for my son and myself that we may eat it and die."*

This woman had not come expecting to meet Elijah at the gate, and had not seen a vision or heard an audible voice from the Lord. In the natural we can say she did not hear anything like an order from God to serve Elijah. When Elijah left for Zarephath, he also did not know exactly how God was going to do it, but just obeyed and went.

Elijah said to her, "Fear not, go and do as you have

What Happens When We Pray and Believe God

said; but first make me a little cake of it and bring it to me and afterwards make for yourself and your son, *"For thus says the Lord the God of Israel, the jar of meal shall not be spent and cruse of oil shall not fail until the day that the Lord shall send rain upon the earth."* And she went and did as Elijah said – for the inner her, was already subject to the command from God, to serve Elijah. That is why she just accepted the word – and she and he and her household ate for many days.

Isaiah 55:8-9 "For my thoughts are not your thoughts, neither are your ways my ways, says the Lord. For as the heavens are higher than the earth, so are my ways higher than your ways and my thoughts than your thoughts."

Thanks be to God, we say, "come let us go up to the mountain of the Lord, to the house of the God of Jacob, that he may teach us his ways and that we may walk in his paths." Isaiah 2:3.

Your part is to believe that you receive it, and God will take care of the rest.

Genesis 24:1 – "Abraham was now very old and the Lord had blessed him in everything he did. Vs2 – He said to his oldest servant who was in charge of all that he had, "place your hand between my thighs and make

As This Happens When We Pray and Believe God

A vow." That he had to get a wife for Isaac from among his relatives. Vs9 So the servant put his hand between the thighs of Abraham, his master, and made a vow to do what Abraham had asked.

The servant took ten of his master's camels and went to the city where Nahor had lived in northern Mesopotamia. Vs11 – When he arrived, he made the camels kneel down at the well outside the city. It was late afternoon the time when women come out to get water.

Vs12 – He prayed, *"Lord, God of my master Abraham, give me success today and keep your promise to my master. Vs13 – Here I am at the well where the young women of the city will be coming to get water. I will say to one of them, "Please lower your jar and let me have a drink."* And if she says, "Drink, and I will also bring water for your camels, may she be the one that you've chosen for your servant Isaac. If this happens, I will know that you have kept your promises to my master."

Vs15 – Before he had finished praying, Rebecca arrived with a water jar on her shoulder. She was the daughter of Bethuel, who was the son of Abraham's brother, Nahbor and his wife Milcah.

She was a very beautiful young girl and still a virgin.

What Happens When We Pray and Believe God

She went down to the well, filled her jar, and came back. Vs17 – The servant ran to meet her and said, "Please give me a drink of water from your jar."

God had already taken over from the moment he prayed. Note that Rebecca had come to fetch water – not to meet Abraham's servant – and after filling the jar she was on the way back home, and there were a number of girls at the well. *The Bible doesn't say that the servant went around asking for that one who had heard the voice of God concerning his mission.* It says, the servant just decided to run and meet Rebecca.

When we pray and believe God, God moves in His way and many times His movements are so different from ours that we may not understand them. *You see, here God caused this servant of Abraham to run and meet the right girl. It might have been a kind of a witness from inside or a spiritual sensation* – whatever it was, the act was right. So, we only need to believe that we receive it, and God will do His part.

Vs18 – She said, "Drink sir," and quickly lowered her jar from her shoulder and held it while he drank. Vs19 – When she had finished she said, "I will also bring water for your camels and let them have all they want." She quickly emptied her jar into the camels' drinking trough and ran to the well to get more water

As This Happens When We Pray and Believe God

Until she had watered all his camels. The man kept watching her in silence to see if the Lord had given him success. Vs26 – Then the man knelt down and worshipped the Lord. Vs27 – He said, *"Praise the Lord, the god of my master Abraham, who has faithfully kept his promise to my master's relative."*

The Lord says, "I am God and always will be. No one can escape from my power; no one can change what I do."

Isaiah 43:13 – Yea, before the day was I am he, and there is none that can deliver out of my hand. I will work, and who shall let it?

God was moving, and in effect the girl acted in line with Abraham's servant's request. So beloved, let the word of God dwell in you richly that you may discern God's will for you. Then pray, believing you receive whatsoever you ask for and you shall have it.

Beloved of God, you are God's child. The day you confessed Jesus Christ as Lord and Saviour of your life, you attained a heavenly position in Christ. You have inherited wealth, wisdom, power and riches with Christ, for you are joint heirs with the Son of God. *"But as it is written: Eye has not seen, nor ear heard, Nor have entered into The heart of man the things*

What Happens When We Pray And Believe God

which God has prepared for those who love Him." I Corinthians 2:9

You have faith, and release that faith by acting on God's Word concerning the desires of your heart, for there is so much for you, yet to bring to manifestation on the earth. That is ask, and it shall be given, seek and you will find, knock and the door will be opened for you.

Things like those documented above happen when we pray and believe God. *What God made happen for others, He is miraculously making happen for you, right now!*

Works of Faith

For as the body without the spirit is dead, so faith without works is dead also. James 2:26

Believing is an act of faith. When you say you have faith in God about something, it implies you are believing God concerning that thing and as a result you have faith as the substance or surety of whatever you have believed God for.

Beloved, real faith cannot lack works, for when a man has faith, it implies that he has a seal that is, he is now ready to be used of God in whatever way concerning

As This Happens When We Pray and Believe God

the issues he has faith for. You know, believing God is like going before God and saying, Lord, I yield to your will that you may do as you please. What I mean is to stop struggling concerning a certain issue and let God completely take over.

When a man believes God, that man is ready to offer anything which the Lord may require of him, i.e., to do anything which the Lord may tell him to do, to use anything which the Lord may tell him to use, to go anywhere the Lord may tell him to go. Believing God is handing it over to God – that is, handing yourself to God, its letting God move without you offering any resistance.

Actually, when one believes God, what He is saying is this, if you need my legs, head, ears, eyes, hand, etc. Lord they are at your service, if you need my money, food, clothes, etc., they are at your disposal. Only say a word and I will act on that.

Beloved of God, when you do believe the Word of God, you receive faith – the substance of what you have believed for and when you have faith it implies that you are in the state of believing. And when you have faith it implies that God has taken over concerning that issue; it's like going to the hotel and paying money for services, then a receipt is given in

What Happens When We Pray and Believe God

return; and you sit at the table with the receipt in your hands. If one asks you why you are seated comfortably though you haven't been served yet, you will show the evidence of what is going on, that is the receipt, which implies that they are working on your order and you are sure they will deliver.

Faith is something from God, and of God – the evidence of the unseen. The substance of things hoped for, and when God takes over, evidently you have whatever you are believing for, because God is Almighty.

We need to understand this very well, for when it is understood, grounds for unbelief will be removed and spirits of unbelief will be conquered.

God is still a creator. He is still on the throne regulating and directing everything.

There is no heart too hard for God to use and there is no creature that can resist His hand. So, when we believe God for something, it implies we have let Him provide in His way – for God says in His word, *"Remember this and show yourselves men, bring it again to mind O ye transgressors, remember the former things of old; for I am God and there is none else; I am God and there is none like me, declaring the end from the beginning and from ancient time the*

As This Happens When We Pray and Believe God

things that are not yet done, saying, my counsel shall stand, and I will do all my pleasure." Isaiah 46:8-10.

The state of our hearts when we believe God is a contrite and humble one towards God, concerning the issue, and God says in His word, *"I dwell in the high and holy place with Him also that is of a contrite and humble spirit, to revive the spirit of the humble and to service the heart of the contrite ones."* Isaiah 57:15.

God says in His word, *"Yea, before the day was I am He and there is none that can deliver out of my hand. I will work and who shall let it/hinder it."* Isaiah 43:13 So beloved when we pray and believe God to answer our prayer, we definitely have whatever our request is and faith is the evidence of it.

So, a faith which is a result of believing God's word can't lack works – that's results.

You know when God first created man, man used to live by trusting God. That's faith in God, but when man got away from believing what God said man is, and what he should do, man fell away from that place of faith in God and became a worker – that is why in a way, things are seemingly hard for man. But, when Jesus Christ came, the trend was reversed to normal. Believers, we are supposed to live by faith – by trust-

What Happens When We Pray and Believe God

ing God – that is going about things as God says and that is really a victorious life.

Believing should not be very complicated, it should be yielding to God wholly-heartedly, a child-like trust letting all bolts loose and the peace which surpasses all understanding then reigns in your heart.

Faith is a real thing you may not touch it with your hands, but it is a substance, something which is tangible spiritually, when you have it you know you have it, and those around you can see it and hear it – actually sense it. It is like when one has a fever. In a way you sense it and realize that it is there.

Faith begins where God's will is known, it is acting on the word of God, receiving the word of God and letting it settle in our hearts.

The word of God is alive/powerful, and whenever it is received and believed there is a change for better. So, a man who has accepted the word of God concerning a certain situation will act according to that word. If a brother or a sister be naked and destitute of daily food and you know and believe (Luke 6:38) "Give and it shall be given unto you, good measure, pressed down and shaken together and running over shall men give into your bosom. For

As This Happens When We Pray and Believe God

With the same measure that you mete withal/deal out it shall be measured to you." Then you won't say to them, depart in peace, be ye warmed and filled, but you will act in faith on the Word of God and that's faith – you have it.

If Ye Be Willing and Obedient Ye Shall Eat The Good of the Land Isaiah 1:19

Malachi 3:6 – "I am the Lord, and I do not change, and so you, the descendants of Jacob are not yet completely lost,…Turn back to me and I will turn to you. But you ask, "What must we do to turn back to you?" I ask you, "Is it right for a person to cheat God?" Of course not, yet you are cheating me. 'How?', you ask. In matters of tithes and offerings. A curse is on all of you because the whole nation is cheating me.

Vs10 – Bring the whole amount of your tithes to the temple so that there will be plenty of food there. Put me to the test and you will see that I will open the windows of heaven and pour out on you in abundance all kinds of good things. Vs11 – I will not let insects destroy your crops and your grape vines will be loaded with grapes. Vs12 – Then the people of all nations will call you happy because your land will be a good place to live. There are certain things in the

What Happens When We Pray and Believe God

Word of God, which when you don't do, you don't sin, but you don't benefit either.

We are at a time whereby there is so much going on. Wickedness is running rampant, devils and demons are running around attacking families, marriages, school children, cities, nations and violence is exercised at amazing and unusual levels all around us. If we ever needed the power of God, and the provisions of God, as well as His protection, we really need it now.

There are some areas where people tend to struggle, especially when it comes to, "what to do" to effectively change the circumstances. For example: the need of a prayer language in regard to intercession. As it is written: *"Likewise the Spirit also helps in our weaknesses. For we do not know what we should pray for as we ought, but the Spirit Himself makes intercession for us with groanings which cannot be uttered. Now He who searches the hearts knows what the mind of the Spirit is, because He makes intercession for the saints according to the will of God."* Romans 8:26-27

We need the help of the Holy Spirit for us to pray effectively regarding the tough times like these whereby so much is at stake.

As This Happens When We Pray and Believe God

In the book of Acts, Peter had a vision, and in that vision a voice came to him from the Lord God Almighty: "And a voice came to him, "Rise, Peter; kill and eat." But Peter said, "Not so, Lord! For I have never eaten anything common or unclean." And a voice spoke to him again the second time. What God has cleansed you must not call common." Acts 10:13-15.

In this case, we see Peter, an apostle of our Lord and Savior Jesus Christ, a believer like you and me, and one who was there on the Day of Pentecost, in the Upper Room among the 120, and was graced to be a partaker of the wonderful experience, of the Baptism of the Holy Spirit, with evidence of speaking in tongues. And was empowered with the anointing to do miracles, wonders and signs, yet he is struggling with the idea of carrying out the divine instruction from the Lord, God Almighty. Simply, "Rise, Peter; kill and eat."

This should not be so with you. God Almighty desires that you willingly receive His promises and provisions, and whatever He says we need, we need it. Beloved, great things happen when we pray and believe God. This is your moment, this is your time, to receive your miracle.

Jehovah-Shammah

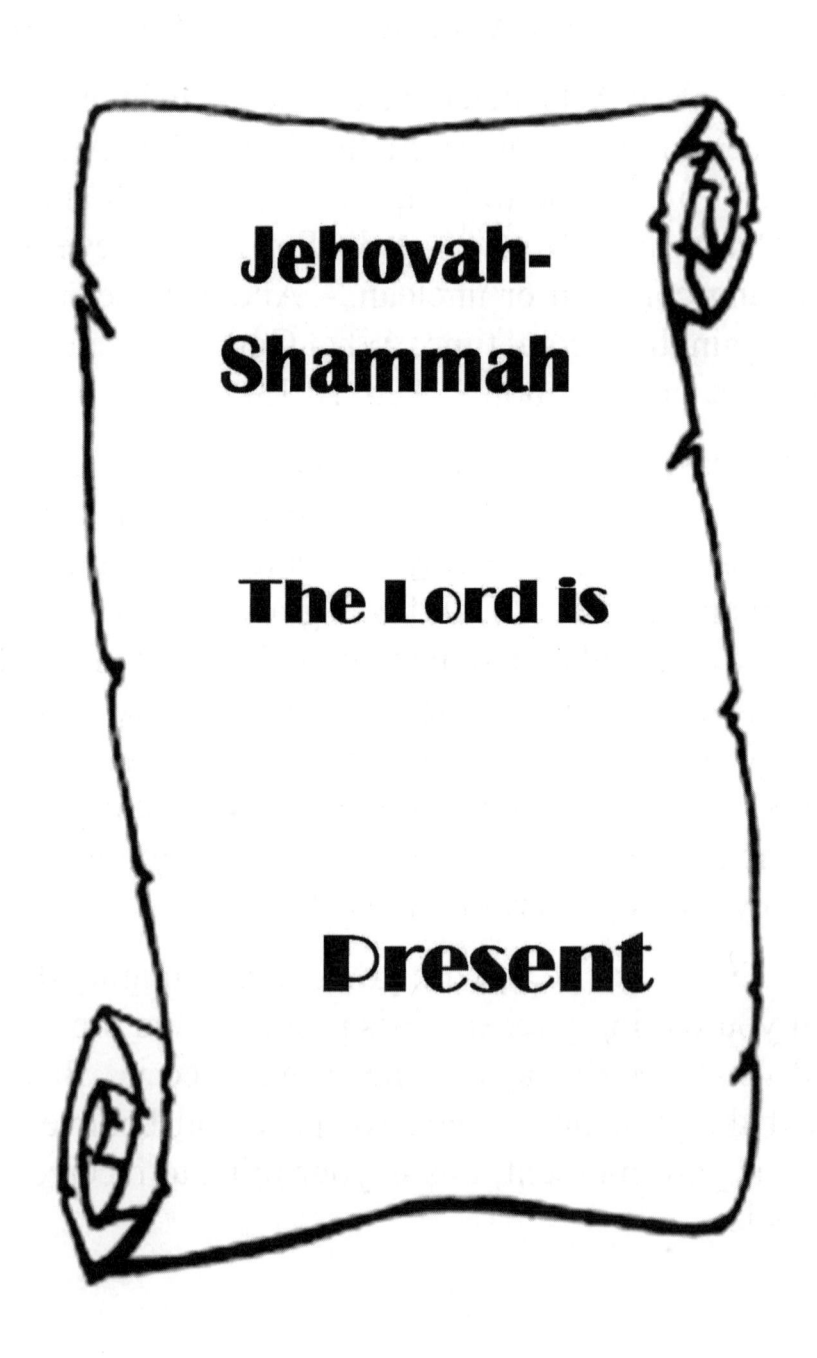

The Lord is Present

FOUNDATIONAL TRUTH V

IS THE SAME YESTERDAY, TODAY AND FOREVER

"Jesus Christ is the same yesterday, today and forever. Hebrews 13:8

Beloved of God, what happened in the Bible times when people prayed and God moved on their behalf is still happening now; for God has never changed and does not change, as the Bible puts it, "In the beginning was the Word, and the Word was with God, and the Word was God.

The same was in the beginning with God" John 1:1-2. So, if the Word – Jesus, does not change, then God does not change, then God does not change either, for the Father, the Son and the Holy Ghost are one.

The Word proceeds from the Father. *"But when the Comforter is come, whom I will send unto you from the Father, even the Spirit of truth, which proceeds from the Father, he shall testify of me."* John 15:26 So, the Holy Spirit proceeds from the Father also.

We are dealing with *Foundational Truth V*, that Jesus

What Happens When We Pray and Believe God

is the same yesterday, today and forever, the things He did while He was here on earth, healing the sick, raising the dead, opening blind eyes, chasing away devils from people's lives, miraculously feeding thousands, He still does today.

It is very important to get understanding in regard to this book of, What Happens When We Pray and Believe God, for Jesus Christ is among us as He said, that where two or three are gathered in my name, that is where I am. Thou we don't see Him with our physical eyes, but He is very present in our midst.

Jesus said, *"And whatever you ask in My name, that I will do, that the Father may be glorified in the Son. If you ask anything in My name, I will do it." John 14:12-14* Here, the Lord emphases the fact that He will do it. Not that somebody else will do it, but Himself, will go out and make things happen for us.

In 1981 when I was studying in Senior Five at St. Henry's College Kitovu in Masaka, Uganda, I happened to escort an aunt to a prayer meeting. The meeting was at Kampala in a place called Nankulabye and there was a man of God who was greatly used of God. To me, it was a very drastic encounter, for all my life I had never seen someone praying and miracles following instantly. This man could cast out

Is the Same Yesterday, Today and Forever

demons in the Name of Jesus Christ. He could lay hands on the sick and they would recover, dumb people had their speech restored, blind ones miraculously received their sight, lame folks had their legs straightened, signs and wonders were taking place.

You know, I was brought up in a Catholic religious background. Uganda by then was predominantly dominated by the Catholic Church and the Anglican Church.

I grew up serving in the Catholic Church. I started serving when I was nine years old. I was what they called an "altar boy," someone who goes before the priest when a mass is being conducted. Every day I would appear in the 5:00pm Mass. I liked the work and the religion so much until I would wait at the church thirty minutes before the bells rang to call the church service to order.

During that period of time, I never knew that God was still active in the earth, as of old times. Oh, yes; during the mass they would read aloud what Jesus used to do when He was here on earth, but I never saw it happening there.

I concluded that not only to me, but it seems all the fellow Catholics thought so in the Church that all

What Happens When We Pray and Believe God

went away with Jesus and the apostles. That is an intelligent man's deduction, and I would say it was in order. So now, here is a man like all other men doing the things which Jesus himself used to do.

My friend, I was really astonished. I had heard Mark 16:17-18 read a number of times at the pulpit in the Catholic Church, *"And these signs shall follow them that believe; In my name shall they cast out devils, they shall speak with new tongues, they shall take up serpents and if they drink any deadly thing, it shall not hurt them; they shall lay hands on the sick and they shall recover."*

It was not new to me. What was new now was seeing someone doing it. My parents were Catholics, and nearly all the relatives also. To say the least about them, for complicated matters, they could easily run to witch doctors for help and you know that it means; it means eating your goats, cows, sheep and losing your money and eventually ending up in hell.

In addition, they could end up serving the devil under the disguise that it is God who put these institutions and gave them power to deliver them. Isn't that a big lie? "Ye are of your father the devil, and the lusts of your father ye will do. He was a murderer from the beginning and abode not in the truth because there is

Is the Same Yesterday, Today and Forever

no truth in him. When he speaks a lie, he speaks of his own: for he is a liar and the father of it." (John 8:44)

The devil has lied to people to the extent of them calling him 'their grandfather' or ancestor! That's how far they went and I grew seeing all of that.

That day, was a great day for me. First of all, I attentively observed everything, to see and be sure about the source of the power, and since I had a very powerful religious background, at least I could make a good judgment concerning some things.

I realized the man was acting on the Word of God, and he was preaching a risen Christ. The only difference I saw between the way he went about it, and the priests at my Catholic Church, was he had a lot of emphasis on the Word of God and he was glorifying Jesus so much, as well as blessing God the Father, and the Son, and miracles then followed.

There was something else special about this man of God. It seemed he was very loving and realistic, very peaceful and joy was on his face and he had a lot of wisdom in the word of God. Definitely, the Spirit of God was in him, as the king of Babylon in Daniel's time observed, "O Belteshzzar (Daniel), master of the magicians, because I know that the Spirit of the holy

What Happens When We Pray and Believe God

gods is in thee and no secret troubleth thee, tell me the visions of my dream that I have seen and the interpretation thereof." Daniel 4:9

The anointing of God was really on him. I saw what the Bible says in Luke 4:18 practically, *"The Spirit of the Lord is upon me, because he hath anointed me to preach the gospel to the poor, he hath sent me to heal the broken hearted, to preach deliverance to the captives, and recovering of sight to the blind, to set at liberty them that are bruised."*

This is what I saw. That day, I saw men and women who had been in prison testifying how they were miraculously released as a result of that man's prayer with their relatives. By then, Uganda was in a very bloody state. A lot of people were being killed by ruthless men.

Many were put in prison without clear offences. Stealing was rampant. Bullets were everywhere. It was really terrible. I heard others testifying of thefts around their homes but only their houses had not been broken into; due to prayer.

It was really glorious and I saw many repenting of their sins and coming into salvation through Christ: as well as receiving the gift of the Holy Spirit. "Then Peter said unto them, repent and be baptized everyone

Is the Same Yesterday, Today and Forever

of you in the Name of Jesus Christ for the remission of sins, and ye shall receive the gift of the Holy Ghost." Acts 2:38. Beloved, people repented and all of them I saw that day, were from the Catholic and Anglican Church.

I was really surprised. They repented and got saved. They confessed salvation. *"For with the heart man believeth unto righteousness; and with the mouth confession is made unto salvation."* Romans 10:10

That is exactly what they did. Beloved, if you are not yet saved but only in religion, please be realistic to yourself and come to Christ the Bible way. It is by grace not works. Thanks to God for the good works. We love them, but we are "Being justified freely by His grace through the redemption that is in Christ Jesus." Romans 3:24

The word of God says, *"If thou shalt believe in thine heart that God raised Him from the dead, thou shalt be saved."* Romans 10:9. So Honey, do that and things will be well with you.

It seemed as if God Himself was right there. In my religious upbringing, I had been taught to be cautious about the last days, for false prophets were to appear and do great miracles and wonders, but there was no true prophet doing wonders and miracles shown to us,

What Happens When We Pray and Believe God

and if you are not careful you may die waiting for the true prophets while they are already in the land. Any way, you can know them – men of God, by their fruits. *"But the fruit of the Spirit is love, joy, peace, long sufferings, gentleness, goodness, faith, meekness, temperance: against such there is no law."* Galatians 5:22-23.

This is what I saw in the people who were there – saved. Beloved, I had seen so much of the other side of the coin. *"Now the works of the flesh are manifest, which are these; adultery, fornication, uncleanness, lasciviousness, idolatry, witchcraft, hatred, variance, emulations, wrath, strife, seditions, heresies, envyings, murders, drunkenness, revellings and such like: of the which I tell you before, as I have also told you in time past that they which do such things shall not inherit the Kingdom of God."* Galatians 5:19-21

You only need to move out fifty meters and come face to face with that; either it is in you or in John, Peter, Catherine, Leonard…. Names given to us at conversion to different religions.

I love them, for those men and women to whom these names belong, received Christ as their personal Savior and I believe many are in heaven, but if your confidence is in the name and religion you may go to hell with both. For those names and religions can not

Is the Same Yesterday, Today and Forever

save a man from the wrath of God for, "Neither is there salvation in any other: for there is none other name under heaven given among men whereby we must be saved." Acts 4:12 except Jesus Christ.

After all that, I decided to get in the line and get to the gentleman, who was now praying for people individually. I got to him, yes; it demanded a lot of patience for the people were many. You know, people can come to their God if the truth is ministered to them.

What the man told me that day surprised me. For, I was not yet saved then, and I was a Catholic (I had my religion).

When he looked at me, joy filled his heart and he prophesied: 'You will pastor and teach God's people; miracles and wonders will accompany your ministry, you will be used of God to build a church and you will write a number of books as the Spirit of God leads you.'

When I heard this, I did not give it much thought, for I could not understand properly what was happening. First of all, I was not sure whether it was true, for I had never thought of being otherwise, except a Catholic, and maybe an engineer as a profession.

What Happens When We Pray and Believe God

Then I asked him to pray for me for we would soon be taking the university entrance exams. He asked me if I had a Bible, to which I replied, "no," for in my religion the Bible was only read at the church, in special readings, and we had never been told to possess it.

The man of God asked me if I had the money to buy one, but I did not have the money either. So he told me he was going to pray that before I reach home, I would have one. He did pray a very short prayer, "Father give Leonard a Bible today before he reaches home in the Name of Jesus Christ I pray: for you said Lord, *'And whatsoever ye shall ask in my name, that will I do, that the Father may be glorified in the Son.'* John 14:13, thank you Father for the Bible."

Then he confidently instructed me to appear with my miracle Bible the next Saturday, and then he would pray for me. Immediately after that service, I headed for home. I had to board two taxi cabs: one from Nnakulabye to the Kampala Park, and the other from the park to Kansanga, where I was living – my home.

The Bible says, "You shall know the truth and the truth shall set you free." John 8:32. I eagerly wanted to see what was going to happen now that the man of

Is the Same Yesterday, Today and Forever

God had prayed and believed God. Remember, this is the topic of this book, "What Happens When We Pray and Believe God."

I took the first taxi home with its first stop at Kampala City Park. There I boarded the one going to Kansanga, and a certain aunt of mine happened to board the same taxi at the same time.

She asked me where I was coming from, and I informed her that I had just come from a church service. Then I told her that the man of God told me to return the next Saturday with the Bible. Hardly had I finished saying it, when suddenly someone in the back seat, asked me if I needed the Bible. I said "yes." Then he told me where he was coming out of the taxi.

It was about hundred meters from where I was going to come out. He said "Please follow me home at the place I am coming out the taxi and I give you a brand new Bible.

I came out with him at that place and he took me to his home and gave me a brand new Bible! I still have it.

The scriptural quotations you are reading are from this Bible. It's a King James Version by the Gideon's. He also asked me to write to him in case there are friends

What Happens When We Pray and Believe God

of mine who need Bibles, and he would send them some.

I reached home with the Bible; as the man of God had prayed. Beloved, pray and believe God, for what God did for me, He is doing the same for you right now. He never changes. "For I am the Lord, I change not, therefore ye sons of Jacob are not consumed." Malachi 3:6 Glory to God! I got the Bible before I reached home.

You may say that I went around looking for it. No, I did not, and when I was talking to my Auntie, I didn't tell her that the man of God had told me I will get a Bible before I reach home. It is God who moved this way.

Let me add this one also, that you may see how God moves. Though I had seen all that and heard God's will for my life through the man of God, I still didn't get saved. I only laid this information in my subconscious and went on with other issues which seemed right in my eye sight. "All the ways of a man are clean in his own eyes; but the Lord weighs the Spirits." Proverbs 16:2 Remember what I had experienced, was a major test of my faith, as it may be with you right now, or it might have been with you long ago. Beloved, the

Is the Same Yesterday, Today and Forever

Lord God Almighty is the Creator of everything. He is the overall king, and He has a right over his creation. You and I are His creation. Thanks be to God; and He has the best for us. *"Thou art worthy O lord to receive glory and honor and power: for thou hast created all things, and for thy pleasure they are and were created,"* Revelations 4:11

God has a vision for his creation. Beloved, God has a vision for each of us. God wills that all of us be saved. He doesn't want any of us to get lost. But, we must respond to His calling, we have to receive His Son, Jesus Christ. *"He that believeth on the Son of God hath the witness in himself; he that believeth not God hath made him a liar; because he believeth not the record that God gave of his Son."* 1 John 5:10.

This is for all of us. Individually there is a perfect will of God for you. He could be making a banker, an engineer, a medical doctor, businessman, carpenter – as Joseph was, lawyer…out of you, and any other good trade from Him. But for me, He wanted to make me a minister of His Word – the Gospel.

I was thinking otherwise for I did not know how someone becomes a preacher, for that was not part of our curriculum in school. You know, child of God,

What Happens When We Pray and Believe God

God is not a man to lie nor son of man to repent, what He says He will see to it that it comes to pass. *"God is not a man that He should lie; neither the son of man that He should repent: hath He said, and shall He not do it? Or hath He spoken and shall He not make it good?"* Numbers 23:19

In my early days, when I was around 11 years of age, the idea of serving God had cropped in my heart, and I had approached the priests of the parish where I used to minister as an altar boy and talked to them about it: they liked the idea for I had told them that I wanted to become a priest.

They had started making arrangements for me to go to Seminary after primary seven, but my parents had to approve of it first. When I asked my mother, she said, "No, you are still too young to make such a vital decision. You need to first grow up and then make an appropriate decision."

Now, without my parent's approval, the priests could not carry out their arrangements to send me to seminar to become a priest. It really grieved me; for I had a burning desire to serve the Lord. I wanted also to put on those long cloaks and go about the altar; I grew up around the altar. I wanted to move from altar boy to

Is the Same Yesterday, Today and Forever

Priest. Doesn't that sound big and exciting? I did not know any better, but glory. "Now unto Him who is able to do exceedingly, abundantly above all that we think or ask, according to the power that worketh in us." Ephesians 3:20 Thanks to God, I did not go there.

I passed the university entrance exams and was accepted as a freshman at Makerere University, Kampala, Uganda - Africa. Remember my interest was engineering and a special kind. I wanted Irrigation and Water Conservation Engineering, which with the recommendation of the Dean of Makerere University, I obtained a Chinese government scholarship, to go to Hahai University, Nanjing, China.

I had to take an exam presented by the Chinese Government in order to obtain their scholarship. God helped me, and I scored very high on the exams, and received a scholarship. The scholarship came as a full package, including tuition and plane fare. Everything the Chinese Government promised to provide, they did, a very nice offer.

Thanks to the Chinese Government, I was to leave Uganda in October of that year, but a few months before I left, I visited my friend Fred. We had started

What Happens When We Pray and Believe God

Together the journey education all the way from Senior One to Six, at St. Henry's College, Kitovu, Masska, Uganda whose motto was, "For Greater Horizons." So we were at this university now, aiming higher to the greater horizons.

I Get Born Again in Lumumba Hall

Fred was saved – born again. "Jesus answered and said unto him, Verily, verily I say unto thee, except a man be born again, he cannot see the Kingdom of God." John 3:3 This brother was for the Kingdom of God, me; I was not yet born again. He was really different from me in the way he went about doing things.

He talked good and many times he glorified Christ. Here, I am in his room at Makerere University in Lumumba Hall. My residence was in Mitchell Hall. Interesting enough, his roommate was also saved.

The moment he saw me, he turned to his friend and started telling him about my love for God and how I go to the Catholic Church every morning and attend the morning mass, but I had never accepted Jesus Christ as my personal savior, according to the scriptures. They both asked me to repent of my sins and accept the Lord Jesus Christ as my personal Lord

Is the Same Yesterday, Today and Forever

and Savior, which I did on my knees, for we all knelt down, and they instructed me to repeat after them; the prayer leading to salvation.

God used Fred, and I came to Christ, but I never fellowshipped with the saved brethren, I did not attend their church services. Instead, I went back to "religion!" But God, had that day started a very good work in me.

When people asked me, "Are you saved?" I could honestly reply, "Yes," but a saved Catholic!

Child of God, there is nothing like that. Salvation is through Jesus Christ only. Never say you are saved in your religion, as I have also heard some Moslems say. When you get saved, you then become a Christian; Christ-like. The Holy Spirit of God takes residence in you and leads you. *"For as many as are led by the Spirit of God, they are the sons of God."* Romans 8:14

From Uganda to China

Anyway, that year I flew to China. While I was there, I strongly joined the Christian fellowship at the University. I also joined by correspondence a Bachelor's degree in Divinity program through I.C.I.

What Happens When We Pray and Believe God

based in Hong Kong. The Lord seriously and in great power spoke to me about His plan and purpose for my life, while I was in China. He confirmed it to me even more through His anointed servants-ministers.

Beloved, don't get in full-time ministry until you are sure the Lord wants you that way. There are hard sailings ahead, and it takes someone who has heard God Himself, speak to him to stay steady.

When He calls you, please respond; don't tell Jesus that 'I have to go and bury my grandfather first,' By the time you are through with burying all of them, you might be too old to do much for God, and a number of others would already be in Hell.

When in my second year of doing Irrigation and Water Conversation Engineering, at Hahai University in Nanjing, China, the Word of the Lord came to me regarding my call:-

The Lord God said to me, *"You shall put the deepest truth into words by revelation knowledge, and many will be drawn to the love of God through the call on your life. Healings will follow, miracles, wonders and signs and many books will be written, and I will send you to nations to preach the Gospel of Peace."* All of this has come to pass in my life.

Is the Same Yesterday, Today and Forever

This was a very interesting encounter, for the understanding I had in the beginning, was that your trade is first, that is the area of your profession. My family, my friends all what they were encouraging me to be was an Irrigation and Water Conservation Engineer, but now someone greater than them, God the Father, had said that I was to be a preacher/pastor.

This book is about what happens when we pray and believe God, and we are dealing with *Foundational Truth IV,* Is the Same Yesterday, Today and Forever, and I am hereby walking you through God's active work through my life as He was making things happen for His people.

You are part of an answer to somebody else's prayer. God Almighty right now is moving you and guiding you into a path that is bringing victory in your life and prosperity in other people's lives. God is omnipotent, omniscient, and omnipresent and is fully able to do what He says He will do.

"The Lord hath prepared His throne in the heavens; and His kingdom ruleth over all." Psalms 103:19

It might be that the Lord has been dealing with you about ministry, to function in the office of an apostle, prophet, evangelist, pastor, or teacher. This is not

What Happens When We Pray and Believe God

Something which a secular university can offer you, nor human beings can deliver, for it is supernatural. It takes the Holy Spirit to point this type of ministerial call out. *"These things we also speak, not in words which man's wisdom teaches but which the Holy Spirit teaches, comparing spiritual things with spiritual. But the natural man does not receive the things of the Spirit of God, for they are foolishness to him; nor can he know them, because they are spiritually discerned."* I Corinthians 2:13-14

I observed that even the twelve apostles of Christ; our Lord Jesus found them busy doing something, but they had to leave those jobs and follow Him.

Matthew had a job. *"And as Jesus passed forth from thence, he saw a man named Matthew sitting at the receipt of custom: and he saith unto him, follow me and he arose and followed him."* Matthew 9:9

He didn't argue with our Lord. He only followed. Peter and the other apostles also forsook things which to them were very valuable; houses, businesses. "Then answered Peter and said unto him, behold we have forsaken all, and followed thee; what shall we have therefore?" Matthew 19:27 Peter wanted to know what the gain was in all this for him. "..., And everyone that hath forsaken houses, or brethren, or sisters, or father, o

Is the Same Yesterday, Today and Forever

mother or wife, or children, or lands, for my name's sake, shall receive an hundred fold and shall inherit everlasting life." Matthew 19:29

God has a blessing for you through your obedience to the call on your life. If you know that you know that God has called you to preach His word within the five-fold office, it is time to obey and prayerfully seek Him for more instructions on what you need to do. This book you are reading today, is a result of my obedience to God and I believe you are being inspired towards your destiny.

A Princess' Life Is Restored

A Princess (sister in Christ) *"But ye are a chosen generation, a royal priesthood, an holy nation, a peculiar people; that ye should shew forth the praises of Him who hath called you out of darkness into His marvelous light."* 1 Peter 2:9, came to me for prayer at the church office in Kampala, Uganda, Africa.

She was a Social Scientist and Administrator, working with the Ministry of Information in Kampala, Uganda. She said, 'Pastor, I am a well-qualified lady, and above all a saved child of God, but things have really turned bad for me. I am staying in a container as a home, with my three children. This container was

What Happens When We Pray and Believe God

never meant for people to live in. It is that storage system designed to store articles that are being shipped. Because I and my three children did not have a place to stay, our only choice was this storage container.

Her husband had died quite some time ago. "We are barely surviving. I asked for a house from the Ministry of Works, where I work, but they had none available." My previous salaries are not yet paid. Though I am well qualified, I haven't been promoted to the place I would want to serve in."

She knew her rights. She quoted Deuteronomy 28:13, "And the Lord shall make thee the head and not the tail: and thou shalt be above only, and thou shalt not be beneath: if that thou harken unto the commandments of the Lord thy God, which I command thee this day, to observe and to do them." This quotation is from the old King James Version of the Bible.

She was wondering why it was not so for her. She was in a very bad state. You could look at her and notice the anxiety. She was hard hit. You could think she was very old, which was not the case. You know, the Devil's job is to make a weary being out of you, but thanks be to God, we can stop the thief. "Submit yourselves therefore to God. Resist the devil and he will flee from you." James 4:7, she had previously enjoyed good positions in the country and tasted the kind of life one should rightfully live.

She had even owned a nice car, and lived in a nice home, with a husband who was a medical doctor, and a well to do man.

Beloved, God wills His children to live well. "For ye know the grace of our Lord Jesus Christ that, "though He was rich, yet for your sakes He became poor, that ye through His poverty might be rich." 2 Corinthians 8:9

You are rich! Not because you have a lot of money with you, not because you have a very big house plus cars, farms, planes, factories. No, you are rich because Jesus became poor and through His poverty you became rich. Now that you are rich, go ahead and acquire your riches by acting on the word of God. *"And this is the confidence that we have in him, that if we ask anything according to his will, he heareth us: and if we know that he hears us, whatsoever we ask we know that we have the petitions that we desired of him."* 1John 5:14-15. The word of God says in III John 2, "Beloved, I wish

What Happens When We Pray and Believe God

above all things that thou mayest prosper and be in health even as thy soul prospereth." So from the Bible we can know God's will concerning our situation, and in this case, it is very clear that God wills that we prosper.

She asked me whether God cares about one's being well. She was so much tossed around by the evil one that she was no longer seeing God according to His word. To her question I told her, 'yes He does care for you' it is the evil one who is causing all these problems in your life, for "The thief cometh not, but for to steal, and to kill and to destroy. I am come that thy might have life and that they might have it more abundantly." John 10:10 says the Lord Jesus Christ.

Thanks be to God, Jesus came and has never changed: so what He said yesterday stands today and forever.

After sharing the Word of God with her for a while, that she may acquire more faith in God, concerning the needs to be met, I then prayed for her. First of all I took authority over the evil one. "Behold, I give unto you power to tread on serpents and scorpions and over all the power of the enemy: and nothing shall by any means hurt you." Luke 10:19. That's the authority I used, you have it also: now that you are born again.

Is the Same Yesterday, Today and Forever

I threw the devil off her; off of her job, out of her house, off of her money and off of her family, for these evil spirits were also causing sicknesses in their bodies.

You know demons do that, they did it to Job, *"So went Satan forth from the presence of the Lord and smote Job with sore boils from the sole of his foot unto his crown."* Job 2:7.

I really, in the Name of Jesus Christ dealt a blow to the devil; the blows that were given to those devils that day were highly effective. I wonder whether the devil knew what hit him! Actually, at the mention of the name Jesus, I could, by the eyes of my Spirit, see demons getting paralyzed and falling off everything belonging to this lady. *"For though we walk in the flesh, we do not war according to the flesh. For the weapons of our warfare are not carnal but mighty in God for pulling down strongholds, casting down arguments and every high thing that exalts itself against the knowledge of God, bringing every thought into captivity to the obedience of Christ, and being ready to punish all disobedience when your obedience is fulfilled."* 2 Corinthians 10:3-11

Beloved, there is power in the Name of Jesus. At this name, demons are rendered powerless and Satan gets

What Happens When We Pray and Believe God

bound. I have seen this happen many times as I minister around the world; God has delivered people from demonic powers in America, Africa, China and Europe. Every time I invoked the Name of Jesus for their deliverance. "Wherefore God also hath highly exalted him and given him a name which is above every name: that at the name of Jesus, every knee should bow, of things in heaven, and things in earth, and things under the earth." Philippians 2:9-10

That's exactly what was happening, and this was a forced bowing. Then I bound the devils in the name of Jesus and threw them in the fiery furnace, with an instruction to never rise again – I mean the demons that were behind all of this mess and confusion in the lady's life. Our Lord Jesus said in Matthew 18:18, "Verily I say unto you, *"Whatsoever ye shall bind on earth shall be bound in heaven; and whatsoever ye shall loose on earth, shall be loosed in heaven."*

So, I knew all heaven was standing by me to justify the noble cause – binding the demons. Child of God, never let the devil play around with your life. You are so precious in the eyes of God. That's why God could allow His son to become sin for you, that you might become the righteousness of God in Christ Jesus. "For He hath made Him to be sin for us, who knew no sin, that we might be made the righteousness of God

Is the Same Yesterday, Today and Forever

in Him." 2 Corinthians 5:21 Therefore, always act when you discern the devil's interaction in your affairs; and he has to obey, for Jesus said, *"And these signs shall follow them that believe; in my name shall they cast out devils, they shall speak with new tongues."* Mark 16:17

Jesus is telling you to act; go ahead and cast the devils out of your situations: also, receive the Baptism of the Holy Ghost and speak in new tongues, now. It is your right, don't abstain from a God-given privilege.

I immediately went to God in prayer and asked in Jesus' name; *"And whatsoever ye shall ask in my name that will I do that the Father may be glorified in the Son."* John 14:13, a house for this lady, money to pay school fees for her children and a promotion on the job, and a new car.

She had informed me that all those with the same academic qualifications as well as experience, had been promoted, except her.

I knew that when God promotes someone, that person's promotion will always materialize in the natural. I asked for the good things she wanted, according to God's will. I was confident and knew my petition had been granted.

Then, with thanksgiving, I concluded the prayer.when

What Happens When We Pray and Believe God

I looked at the princess – daughter of God, she was beaming with joy. To me, that was a sign of agreement; that she had believed.

The meeting was not planned by me nor her, or anyone else. I happened to be on my way home when a thought came in my spirit, that there was a need for me to visit with my sister in Christ. I felt that there was an urgency to see her.

I had to walk half of a kilometer, and my body was tired, it did not want to go, but it was quite a strong conviction from God, until I decided to act on it.

Maybe you are wondering, "What was that that was prompting me?" Thanks be to God, I am a Child of God, and can be led by the Spirit of God, *"For as many as are led by the Spirit of God are the sons of God."* Romans 8:14

This was the Holy Spirit leading. Talking from the natural perspective, I did not want to go, but anyway, I went. When I arrived there, I found the lady I went to visit, but hardly had I spent two minutes with the family when the lady who needed deliverance came in.

This book is about what happens when we pray and believe God, and we are dealing with Foundational Truth IV. Is the same yesterday, today and forever,

Is the Same Yesterday, Today and Forever

You are already noticing in this narrative, that God's hand is actively directing the events that are leading to victory in the lives of the people.

The moment she stepped in the sitting room, my host happily started introducing me to her and told her to counsel with me. Now, realize this: my going to that place was due to God working on the answer as a result of that woman's past prayers. Though she was wondering whether Jesus cared for her at all, the truth was even to me, of whom she was expressing her discontents; I was sent by God to her.

After one month, the lady in whose house we met and prayed, met me again. She said, "Pastor Leonard, the lady you prayed for last time has been looking for you. She left me with her address of the new house she got."

A few days later, I happened to call on her at her new home. I went through two gates. It was really a nice house. She told me that two days after I prayed with her, a sister in Christ happened to talk in her presence about a house she was soon leaving to go to London; for the Lord had sent her to go and minister there. So, she was looking for someone to take over her house, and that person had to be born again, and would also be paying the rent. She also had two relatives of hers

What Happens When We Pray and Believe God

who she wanted to stay in the home with her for some time, until they get a place to move to. Good enough, they were children of God also, for they had received Christ as their personal savior. "But, as many as received Him, to them gave He power to become the sons of God, even to them that believed on His name." John 1:12.

When she was saying all of this, she had not known that right in front of her was a lady seeking and looking for a house. So, the princess took the offer, and was happily left in that nice house.

The government ministry, where she was employed, started paying the rent for her. This took place in early 1990; when getting a house in the City of Kampala, was not easy, for many buildings had been hit by bombs, due to the successive wars in the country, and Uganda was just beginning to build afresh.

We were praying and God was healing the land, "..., and pray one for another that ye may be healed. The effectual fervent prayer of a righteous man availeth much." James 5:16

Our sister received the house within two days after the prayer. Previously she had knocked on many doors looking for a house, and found none. I am not saying

Is the Same Yesterday, Today and Forever

it is wrong to search, but I want you to realize, it is not by power and it is not by the might of a man that caused these things to happen. "Then he answered and spake unto me saying, this is Zerubbabel, saying, Not by might, nor by power, but by my Spirit, saith the Lord of hosts." Zechariah 4:6.

This is what I am bringing to your attention. God can move in an unexpected way for you to receive your miracle. Expect a miracle today, in the Name of Jesus!

This lady lived happily in the house with her school-aged children. A firm that she had worked for in the past, had reevaluated her previous salary and discovered that she had been underpaid. They immediately wrote a check with quite a nice figure on it, to compensate her for their under payment.

She was really surprised! First of all, she did not know that she had been under paid. She took what they gave her thankfully; only to learn that later there was more money for her.

Glory to God! That is the Spirit of God causing things to happen; God answering prayers. She was also promoted on her job to a higher paying position. Beloved, when we pray and believe God, such things as this happens on your behalf!

What Happens When We Pray and Believe God

A Prince Receives Total Healing

In 1988, I met a prince (brother in Christ), an economist, who had studied economics at Makerere University. He had previously worked in Kenya, now he was working in Uganda at a prominent firm, as their Chief Accountant.

His employer laid him off the job, and it happened at the time when he had just gotten married. He was fellowshipping with one of the Full Gospel churches in Kampala. At that time, I was co-pastor in one of those churches.

The Full Gospel Mission Churches in Uganda were quite a big blessing to me. I learned a lot while ministering in many of their churches. I would preach and teach almost every Sunday at the various church locations, which enabled me to share the Word of God, as well as pray for a lot of people. That is where I met this precious brother in Christ Jesus.

This child of God, was going through a very difficult time in his life. He had spent money on his wedding, and here he is now with a wife, and no job. He had looked for employment, and found none. He even crossed over to Kenya, but failed to find one there.

The owner of the house where he stayed, wanted him out because the rent was already past due. So, he had

Is the Same Yesterday, Today and Forever

to move out. The wife had given birth to a baby, but while he was in Kenya looking for a job, a fire broke out at home due to bad connections in the wiring system, and the baby was burned over fifty percent of its body. He was admitted to the hospital in a very severe state.

Nearly half of the property was burned. The devil had really come in like a flood and the brother was in total distress. But his heart was crying out to God for a miracle. He wanted to get out of the net the enemy had laid out for him. *"Put me out of the net that they have laid privily for me: for thou art my strength"*. Psalms 31:4

I happened to visit him at his home, and I learned all that was going on in his life. He told me that a number of people had come to him with condemnation on their lips. They were only telling him why all that had happened, but not helping him get out of it.

Saints, always stay on God's side. *"But if ye had known what this meaneth, I will have mercy, and not sacrifice ye would not have condemned the guiltless."* Matthew 12:7.

This gentleman did not need a judge then, for the whole family could starve while one is still judging:

What Happens When We Pray and Believe God

He only wanted a solution to all the mess. *"He shall call upon me and I will answer him: I will be with him in trouble, I will deliver him and honor him."* Psalms 91:15

That's exactly what he needed: someone who could come in agreement with him to call upon the Lord. He was severely beaten by the Devil. Someone had to stand with him in faith and hold his hands up for victory.

Thanks be to God for the love of the brethren; that even amidst that intense attack by the Devil, God through different brethren, supplied the family's basic needs. "And my God shall supply all your need according to His riches in glory by Christ Jesus." Philippians 4:19

It was so serious; the newly married wife had started complaining about the house. She was fully convinced that demons were in there to kill the whole family. *"The thief cometh not but to steal, kill and to destroy. I have come that they may have life, and that they may have it more abundantly.*" John 10:10 She very urgently wanted to leave that house.

You see, in this case, the Devil had "raised a lot of dust." She was suffocating. Now, I ministered to my

Is the Same Yesterday, Today and Forever

brother the Word of God, so that his faith might increase, for faith cometh by hearing and hearing by the word of God. *"So then faith cometh by hearing and hearing by the word of God."* Romans 10:17.

Through the word of God, he started setting his eyes off the calamities and trials, and focused on the unseen – the principles of God's word.

This is very important, for, until it is so, you won't be in agreement when praying. I wanted him to come in agreement with me. He had to get a proper image of himself through the Word of God. There was a lot of wrong thinking and wrong belief, which we had to cast down. *"Casting down imaginations and every high thing that exalteth itself against the knowledge of God, and bringing into captivity every thought to the obedience of Christ."* 2 Corinthians 10:5

Actually, the Holy Spirit showed me how to do it. Before I came to the help of this child of God, many had told me that he could not be helped, but he Lord commanded me to go to his assistance and I knew these afflictions were coming to an end. "For our light afflictions, which is but for a moment worketh for us a far more exceeding and eternal weight of glory: while we look not at the things which are seen, but at the things which are not seen: for the things which

Happens When We Pray and Believe God

Are ...en are temporal, but the things which are not seen are eternal." 2 Corinthians 4:17-18. I want you to remember that we are dealing with Foundational Truth IV. Is the same yesterday, today and forever.

Right now, the Lord God Almighty is stirring your inner being, to reach out for the best that God has for you through His Son, Jesus Christ. You are the righteousness of God; Christ has become your wisdom and redemption, and you are a prince/princess with God.

Wrestling with God

I do hereby want to bring your attention to what happened in Genesis 32, where Jacob whose name meant: sup planter; trickster, liar, etc. wrestled with the Lord, and in that encounter, because of his persistence and desire to be blessed, God Almighty changed his name to Israel, which means, "Prince with God."

This brother in Christ had received Jesus Christ as his personal Savior, so he had conversion into a new creation. It is like, he wrestled out of wickedness and sin, and he prevailed, resulting in becoming a child of God, a new creation. The Bible says, in Romans 8:1"There is therefore now no condemnation to those

Is the Same Yesterday, Today and Forever

who are in Christ Jesus, who do not walk according to the flesh, but according to the Spirit." He was not under judgment by God. It was not God who was causing all the problems that he was encountering, but it was the enemy, and we had to bind the Devil.

I handed him a book, "How to be Led by the Spirit of God," authored by Rev. Kenneth E. Hagin: a very helpful book. He started reading the book and he quickly started advancing in the Spirit of God.

You have to understand that the Ministry of the Written Word is very, very important, because books can get to places that preachers will never go. I mean the authors. A book like this one, "What Happens When We Pray and Believe God," is a gem in your hands, and should be treasured, for I wrote it under the unction of the Holy Spirit, and I believe it is part of an answer to your prayers.

One Sunday, this man and I sat down to do some real praying. I led the prayer and his faith had increased so much, until it was very easy for him to agree with me. We took authority over the situation, we tied up the devil in the name of Jesus Christ, and cast him off the family. *"Behold, I give you the authority to trample on serpents and scorpions, and over all the power of the enemy, and nothing shall by any means*

What Happens When We Pray and Believe God

hurt you." Luke 10:19. We then went forward to break the hands of the enemy off his job, house and money.

We dispelled the dark cloud which was hovering over their lives, and believed the devil was gone, and gone by force. *"For verily I say unto you, that whosoever shall say unto this mountain, be thou removed and be thou cast into the sea, and shall not doubt in his heart, but shall believe that those things which he saith shall come to pass, he shall have whatsoever he saith."* Mark 11:23.

You know the devil never wants to go. One must always force it to leave.

Glory to God! We have the power to do it. The prince believed that he had been delivered when we prayed, and the shackles of the enemy were broken, and was now ready to receive from God. Then, in the Name of Jesus Christ of Nazareth, the anointed one, I claimed a job for him, a big nice house and healing for the family. *"How God anointed Jesus of Nazareth with the Holy Ghost and with power: who went about doing good, and healing all that were oppressed of the devil: for God was with him."* Acts 10:38

Remember, he had applied for a job at numerous places and received none. However, on the following

Is the Same Yesterday, Today and Forever

Tuesday, he happened to be walking on one of the streets in Kampala, and while there a thought came to him to visit the Uganda Coffee Marketing Board house – Amber House. This was an inner witness in his Spirit.

When he arrived there, he learned that there were some job openings, and among them was an Accountant position. He immediately filled out an application and submitted it for consideration.

Shortly after, he was called for an interview, which he passed, along with other applicants, and he was hired for the position. He was told to find a house and that they would pay the rent as part of his employment package.

He and I found the house, which had a large yard, it was a nice house, and the beautiful thing about it, the Coffee Marketing Board accepted it and immediately rented it for him. Many of his fellow workers were in awe beholding this miracle, for he acquired the house in a very short time.

Shortly after taking the job, the Coffee Marketing Board decided to promote some of its workers to positions abroad. Amazing enough, he was among those chosen. It was really a miracle, for there was

What Happens When We Pray and Believe God

a difference of opinion among the selection committee, for he was newly hired, thou he was highly qualified.

Beloved, it was God who moved when we prayed and believed. "Therefore, I say unto you, what things so ever ye desire, when ye pray, believe that ye receive them, and ye shall have them." Mark 11:24

God has more than a million ways to make things Happen: But as it is written: *"Eye has not seen, nor ear heard, nor have entered into the heart of man the things which God has prepared for those who love Him."* I Corinthians 2:9

Please be a partner to this ministry by sowing your seed in this good ground, that we may get this message to as many as possible.

Honor the Lord with your possessions and with the first fruits of all your increase; so your barns will be filled with plenty, and your vats will overflow with new wine. Proverbs 3:9-10

Many have done that and God
Has healed them miraculously

Leonard Kayiwa Ministries

P.O. Box 1898

Bolingbrook, Illinois 60440

(224)440-6992

kayiwaministries@yahoo.com

THE ISAIAH 58 BLESSING:

You can also receive a copy of this book for a donation of $20.00 or more in support of the drive to help orphans.

Bishop Leonard MP Kayiwa founded a 501©3 tax exempt church organization for helping orphans in different countries in Africa.

This organization is registered in the U.S.A. and in Africa. It is called:

AFRICAN CHILDREN BENEVOLENCE FOUNDATION INTERNATIONAL, INC.

We shall send you a tax-deductible receipt for your gift towards helping God's children – the orphans.

We will also send you a copy of this beautiful book.

Make your check payable to:

A.C.B.F.I., Inc. or African Children Benevolence Foundation International, Inc.

P.O. Box 1898, Bolingbrook, IL 60440

www.acbfii.org; www.ministeringtogod.com

acbfii@yahoo.com   God bless you!!!

"Ekyo kye kirungi, ekikkirizibwa mu maaso g'Omulokozi waffe Katonda, 4 ayagala abantu bonna okulokoka, era okutuuka mu kutegeerera ddala amazima. 5 Kubanga waliwo Katonda omu, era omutabaganya wa Katonda n'abantu omu, omuntu Kristo Yesu, 6 eyeewaayo abe omutango olwa bonna; okutegeeza kulibaawo mu ntuuko zaakwo:" 1Timoseewo 2:3-6

This is Luganda language (Uganda) Africa

"NAYE BWOGERA BUTYA? NTI, EKIGAMBO KIRI KUMPI NAAWE, MU KAMWA KO, NE MU MUTIMA GWO: KYE KIGAMBO EKY'OKUKKIRIZA KYE TUBUULIRA: 9 KUBANGA BW'OYATULA YESU NGA YE MUKAMA N'AKAMWA KO, N'OKKIRIZA MU MUTIMA GWO NTI KATONDA YAMUZUUKIZA MU BAFU, OLIROKOKA: 10 KUBANGA OMUNTU AKKIRIZA NA MUTIMA OKUWEEBWA OBUTUUKIRIVU, ERA AYATULA NA KAMWA OKULOKOKA." Abaruumi 10:8-10

"Naye bonna abaamusembeza yabawa obuyinza okufuuka abaana ba Katonda, be bakkiriza erinnya lye" Yokkaana 1:12

3 Hili ni zuri, nalo lakubalika mbele za Mungu Mwokozi wetu;
4 ambaye hutaka watu wote waokolewe, na kupata kujua yaliyo kweli.
5 Kwa sababu Mungu ni mmoja, na mpatanishi kati ya Mungu na wanadamu ni mmoja, Mwanadamu Kristo Yesu;
6 ambaye alijitoa mwenyewe kuwa ukombozi kwa ajili ya wote, utakaoshuhudiwa kwa majira yake.   1 Timotheo Mlango 2:3-6

Swahili Language, Africa

8 Lakini yanenaje? Lile neno li karibu nawe, katika kinywa chako, na katika moyo wako; yaani, ni lile neno la imani tulihubirilo.
9 Kwa sababu, ukimkiri Yesu kwa kinywa chako ya kuwa ni Bwana, na kuamini moyoni mwako ya kuwa Mungu alimfufua katika wafu, utaokoka.
10 Kwa maana kwa moyo mtu huamini hata kupata haki, na kwa kinywa hukiri hata kupata wokovu. Warumi Mlango 10: 8-10

12 Bali wote waliompokea aliwapa uwezo wa kufanyika watoto wa Mungu, ndio wale waliaminio jina lake;   Yohana Mlango 1: 12

3　　　　　　　　　　　　这是好的，在神我们救主面前可蒙悦纳。
4　　　　　　　　　　　　　　他愿意万人得救，明白真道。
5 因为只有一位神，在神和人中间，只有一位中保，乃是降世为人的基督耶稣。
6 他舍自己作万人的赎价。到了时候，这事必证明出来。　　　提摩太前书 2 章 3-6

8 他到底怎么说呢？他说，这道离你不远，正在你口里，在你心里。就是我们所传信主的道。
9　　　　你若口里认耶稣为主，心里信神叫他从死里复活，就必得救。
10 因为人心里相信，就可以称义。口里承认，就可以得救。　　　罗马书 10 章 8-10

12 凡接待他的，就是信他名的人，他就赐他们权柄，作神的儿女。　　約翰福音 1 章 12

Chinese Language

1 Tim 2: 3-6

Fun eyi ni o dara o si ṣe itẹwọgbà ni niwaju Ọlọrun Olugbala wa ti o ba f gbogbo awọn ọkunrin lati wa ni fipamọ ati lati wa si imo ti otitọ. Nitori jẹ ọkan Ọlọrun ati ọkan Onilaja kan pẹlu larin Ọlọrun ati enia, awọn ọkunrin Kristi Jesu, ẹniti fi ara irapada fun gbogbo, lati wa ni jẹri ni nitori akoko.

Yoruba Language   (Nigerian) Africa

John 1:12
Sugbon bi ọpọlọpọ bi gba Re, wọn o fi agbara fun lati di ọmọ Ọlọrun, fun awọn ti o gbà orukọ rẹ.

Rom 10: 9-11

Ti o ba ti o ba jewo pẹlu ẹnu rẹ Oluwa Jesu ki o si gbagbo ninu okan re pe Olorun ti jí i dide kuro ninu okú, o yoo wa ni fipamọ. Nitori pẹlu awọn ọkàn ọkan gbagbo fun ododo, ati pẹlu ẹnu fi ijẹwọ si igbala. Nitori iwe-mimọ wipe, "Ẹniti o ba gbà on u yoo wa ko le fi si itiju".

1 Tim. 2: 3-6
Domin wannan abu ne mai kyau da kuma m, a wurin Allah Mai Cetonmu, yanã nufin dukkan mutane su sami ceto su kuma kai ga sanin gaskiya. Gama akwai Allah daya, matsakanci daya kuma tsakanin Allah da mutane, da mutumin Almasihu Yesu, wanda ya ba da kansa fansa saboda duk, za a shaida a saboda lokaci.

Hausa Language   (Nigeria) Africa

John 1:12
Amma kamar yadda mutane da yawa kamar yadda aka gare Shi, to ya ba su ikon zama 'ya'yan Allah, da wadanda suka yi īmãni, a cikin sunansa.

Rom 10: 9-11
Wannan idan ka furta da bakinka Yesu Ubangiji ne da kuma gaskata a zuciyarka Allah ya tashe shi daga matattu, za ka sami ceto. Domin tare da zuciya daya ya yi īmãni a gare adalci, kuma da baki yake shaidawa ya sami ceto. Domin Nassi ya ce, "Duk wanda ya yi īmãni a gare Shi ba zai kunyata".

1 Tim 2: 3-6
N'ihi na nke a bụ ezi ihe na ihe-anabata n'anya Chineke Nzọpụta anyị na-achọ ka mmadụ nile ka ndị mmadụ na a ga-azoputa na-abịa ka ihe ọmụma nke eziokwu. N'ihi na e nwere otu Chineke na otu onye ogbugbo n'etiti Chineke na mmadụ, onye Christ Jesus, onye nyere onwe Ya ka ihe mgbapụta maka ihe niile, na-gbara akaebe na mgbe oge ruru.

Ibo Language

John 1:12
Ma dị ọtụtụ dị ka natara Ya, ha ka O nyere ike ighọ umu Chineke, ndị kwere n'aha-Ya.

Rom 10: 9-11
Nke ahụ ma ọ bụrụ na ị na-ekwupụtara na ọnụ gị na Onyenwe anyị Jizọs ma kwere na obi gị na Chineke mere ka O si na ndi nwuru anwu, ị ga-azọpụta. N'ihi na-eji obi kwere rue ezi omume, na-ejikwa onu kwuputa rue nzoputa. N'ihi na Akwụkwọ Nsọ kwuru, sị, "Onye ọ bụla nke kwere na Ya, agaghi-eme ka ihere mee".